MONTRÉAL &
QUÉBEC CITY
ENCOUNTER

REGIS ST LOUIS

Montréal & Québec City Encounter

Published by Lonely Planet Publications Pty Ltd
ABN 36 005 607 983

Australia	Head Office, Locked Bag 1, Footscray, Vic 3011
	☎ 03 8379 8000 fax 03 8379 8111
	talk2us@lonelyplanet.com.au
USA	150 Linden St, Oakland, CA 94607
	☎ 510 250 6400
	toll free 800 275 8555
	fax 510 893 8572
	info@lonelyplanet.com
UK	2nd fl, 186 City Rd London EC1V 2NT
	☎ 020 7106 2100 fax 020 7106 2101
	go@lonelyplanet.co.uk

This title was commissioned in Lonely Planet's Oakland office and produced by: **Commissioning Editor** Jennye Garibaldi **Coordinating Editors** Angela Tinson, Alison Ridgway **Coordinating Cartographer** Valeska Canas **Coordinating Layout Designer** Carlos Solarte **Assisting Cartographers** Ross Butler, Joanne Luke, Jacqueline Nguyen **Assisting Layout Designer** Cara Smith **Managing Editors** Brigitte Ellemor, Sasha Baskett **Managing Cartographer** Alison Lyall **Cover research** Naomi Parker, lonelyplanetimages.com **Project Manager** Glenn van der Knijff **Managing Layout Designer** Laura Jane **Thanks to** Jessica Boland, Sally Darmody, Ryan Evans, Joshua Geoghegan, Aomi Hongo, Jim Hsu, Margie Jung, Indra Kilfoyle, Wayne Murphy, Raphael Richards

ISBN 978 1 74179 055 9

Printed through Colorcraft Ltd, Hong Kong.
Printed in China.

Acknowledgment Many thanks for the use of the following content: Montréal Métro Map © STM 2009. Reproduction of this document, in whole or in part, is prohibited without the written authorization of the Société de transport de Montréal (STM).

Lonely Planet and the Lonely Planet logo are trademarks of Lonely Planet and are registered in the US Patent and Trademark Office and in other countries.

Lonely Planet does not allow its name or logo to be appropriated by commercial establishments, such as retailers, restaurants or hotels. Please let us know of any misuses: www.lonelyplanet.com/ip.

© Lonely Planet 2009. All rights reserved.

Mixed Sources
Product group from well-managed forests and other controlled sources
www.fsc.org Cert no. SGS-COC-005002
© 1996 Forest Stewardship Council
FSC

HOW TO USE THIS BOOK
Color-Coding & Maps

Color-coding is used for symbols on maps and in the text that they relate to (eg all eating venues on the maps and in the text are given a green knife and fork symbol). Each neighborhood also gets its own color, and this is used down the edge of the page and throughout that neighborhood section.

Shaded yellow areas on the maps denote 'areas of interest' – for their historical significance, their attractive architecture or their great bars and restaurants. We encourage you to head to these areas and just start exploring!

Although the authors and Lonely Planet have taken all reasonable care in preparing this book, we make no warranty about the accuracy or completeness of its content and, to the maximum extent permitted, disclaim all liability arising from its use.

Send us your feedback We love to hear from readers – your comments help make our books better. We read every word you send us, and we always guarantee that your feedback goes straight to the appropriate authors. The most useful submissions are rewarded with a free book. To send us your updates and find out about Lonely Planet events, newsletters and travel news visit our award-winning website: *lonelyplanet.com/contact*

Note: We may edit, reproduce and incorporate your comments in Lonely Planet products such as guidebooks, websites and digital products, so let us know if you don't want your comments reproduced or your name acknowledged. For a copy of our privacy policy visit *lonelyplanet.com/privacy*

REGIS ST LOUIS

A longtime admirer of the free-spirited ethos that rules Québec, Regis pays frequent visits to Montréal and Québec City. During research on this book, he mounted his bike and logged hundreds of kilometers along Montréal's (generally) bike-friendly streets, visiting the latest restaurants, galleries and bars around town. He has written over two dozen guides for Lonely Planet, and his articles have appeared in the *Los Angeles Times* and the *Chicago Tribune,* among other publications. He lives in New York City, but often daydreams of pulling up stakes and moving to the Plateau.

REGIS' THANKS

Big thanks to Roger, who generously hosted me during my extended sojourn in Montréal. Many thanks to Simona for invaluable contributions to the nightlife, shopping and arts sections. I'd also like to thank Tim Hornyak, Frederic Morin, Dimitri Antonopoulos, Tom Lansky, Eric Khayat, Daniel Weinstock and the Chinatown volleyball team (and their friends and partners) for insight into 'the last great bohemian city in North America.' As always, thanks to Cassandra and Magdalena for continued love and support.

SIMONA RABINOVITCH

A journalist born and raised in Montréal, Simona has written for the *Globe & Mail* as well as *Nylon, Interview* and *Spin.* After living in California, Israel, New York and Toronto, she's back in her hometown writing her first book. Simona contributed to the Shop and Play sections of this book.

THE PHOTOGRAPHER

Photography and travel quench the same thirst for adventure that led Guylain Doyle to move to Montréal in 1987, where he lived for nearly 20 years. In a way, working on this book was kind of like going back home.

Cover photograph Cyclist passing through the Old Town, Québec City, Johanna Huber/4Corners Images.
Internal photographs p47, p62, p68, p90 by Regis St Louis; p142 steve bly / Alamy; p66 Tibor Bognar / Alamy; p140 ColsMontreal / Alamy; p95 Jeff Greenberg / Alamy; p97 Michael Matthews / Alamy; p22 Francis Vachon / Alamy. All other photographs by Lonely Planet Images, and by Guylain Doyle except p13, p100 Olivier Cirendini; p30, p60, p30 Brian Cruickshank; p56, p108, p112 Richard Cummins; p21 Lee Foster; p27 Rick Gerharter; p52, p61, p64, p76, p107, p134 Ray Laskowitz; p14, p24, Glenn van der Knijff; p42 Wayne Walton

All images are copyright of the photographers unless otherwise indicated. Many of the images in this guide are available for licensing from **Lonely Planet Images:** lonelyplanetimages.com

Select from the freshest local fruit at Marché Atwater (p49)

CONTENTS

Why is our travel information the best in the world? It's simple: our authors are passionate, dedicated travelers. They don't take freebies in exchange for positive coverage so you can be sure the advice you're given is impartial. They travel widely to all the popular spots, and off the beaten track. They don't research using just the internet or phone. They discover new places not included in any other guidebook. They personally visit thousands of hotels, restaurants, palaces, trails, galleries, temples and more. They speak with dozens of locals every day to make sure you get the kind of insider knowledge only a local could tell you. They take pride in getting all the details right, and in telling it how it is. Think you can do it? Find out how at **lonelyplanet.com**.

THIS IS MONTRÉAL & QUÉBEC CITY

History and culture collide in two of North America's most dynamic destinations. Montréal and Québec City embody the spirit for which their province is famed: its *joie de vivre,* heady French culinary traditions and determination to always follow its own course.

Separatism may no longer be the hot topic it was a decade ago, but no visitor can doubt that these two cities have carved themselves a unique cultural landscape. Gateway to Québec is Montréal, a city whose dual French and English background – plus immigrant communities from across the globe – has created a fascinating blend of cultures. On a typical night in Montréal, music enthusiasts are out listening to French *chanson* (folk singing), big-band jazz and prog rock, while art lovers mix at openings of the latest European, québécois and American exhibitions. Cineasts are lining up for a revival of new-wave cinema, or popping in for the latest indie feature.

The dining scene is no less diverse, with new talented young chefs competing for top honors. You'll find French bistros, Jewish delis, Italian trattorias, steakhouses and Cantonese dining rooms, plus fantastic restaurants serving up Thai, Vietnamese, Lebanese, West African and more.

While lacking the cosmopolitan charms of its big brother, Québec City has obvious appeal. The Old Town is pure eye candy, its laneways sprinkled with 18th-century houses and lovely plazas, while jewel-box churches and the imposing fortress rise above it on the cliffs overlooking the St-Lawrence.

In addition to their urban charms, both cities offer easy access to the outdoors. There are bike lanes crisscrossing Montréal, a lush park on the city's iconic 'mountain', and kayaking along the Canal de Lachine. In Québec City, you can join the great outdoor migration in the historic Battlefields Park.

Top left The impressive hand-carved interior of Basilique Notre-Dame (p12), Old Montréal **Top right** Montréal's iconic Biosphère (p106) on Île Ste-Hélène **Bottom** Succulent regional fruits for sale at Marché Atwater (p49)

>HIGHLIGHTS

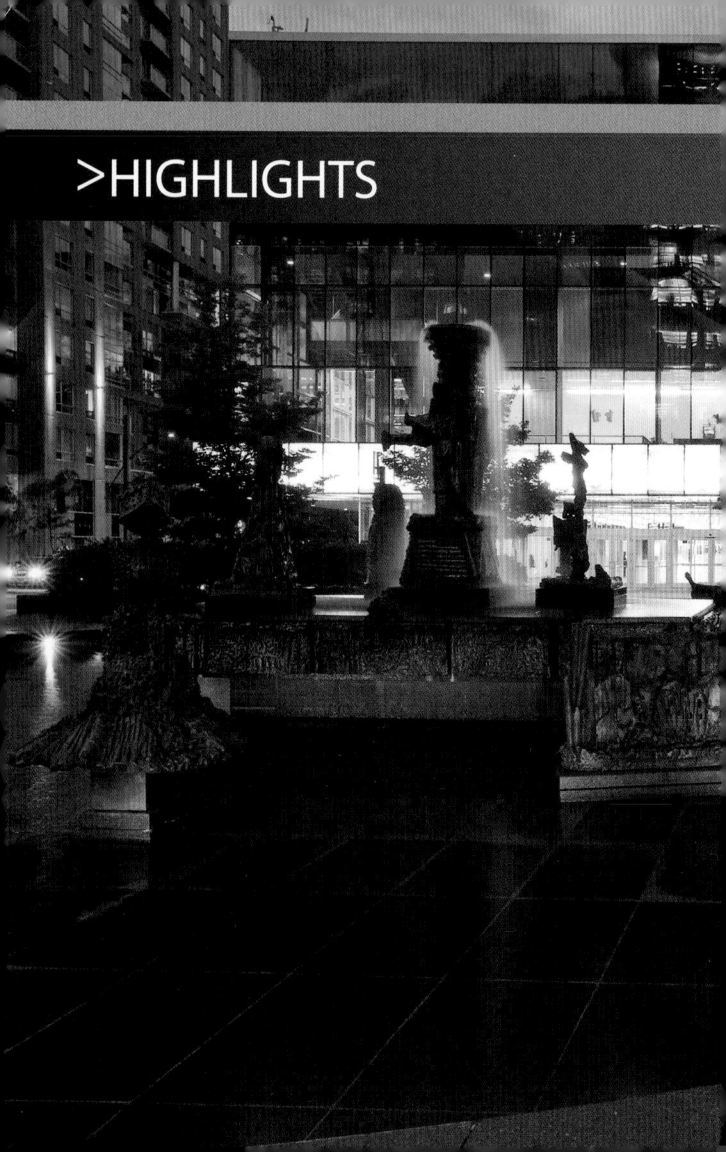

Place Jean-Paul-Riopelle, Old Montréal

>1 OLD MONTRÉAL

WANDER THE COBBLESTONED STREETS OF OLD EUROPE IN THE NEW WORLD

A wander through the cobblestoned streets of this atmospheric quarter takes you back in time, to the earliest days of France's fledgling colony in the New World. History lurks around every corner, from the photogenic stone buildings along the waterfront to the archaeological crypts beneath the city's former Customs House. Here you'll find icons like the Marché Bonsecours (pictured right), a sprawling neoclassical building once housing the city's main marketplace, and the grand Hôtel de Ville (City Hall), where in 1967 French leader Charles de Gaulle fired the dreams of separatists by shouting *'Vive le Québec libre!'* (Long live a free Québec) to the crowds down below.

The crossroads of rough-and-tumble fur traders of the 1600s later became a landscape of winding, narrow lanes dominated by church steeples. Mark Twain once famously remarked that it was 'the first time I was ever in a city where I couldn't throw a brick without breaking a church window.' Indeed its picture-book chapels and grand basilica are symbols of the once dominant French Catholic influence in the area.

The city for its part has taken great pains to preserve this historic district. For its efforts, it has reaped a grand tourist trade – with visitors from all parts coming to soak up a bit of old-world Europe slapped down in North America. In summer, its public plazas and parks take on a carnivalesque atmosphere. Lively Place Jacques-Cartier, with its outdoor bistros and cafes becomes an impromptu stage for the city's most ambitious buskers.

Yet, far from being a static playground for kitsch-loving tourists, Old Montréal has its lures for more discerning visitors as well. New boutique hotels have opened their doors in recent years, along with a crop of imaginative restaurants concealed in the district's narrow back lanes – some hidden in old stone cellars. High-end art galleries and eclectic boutiques cater to the well-heeled residents who've moved into converted lofts around the area. In the evening, visitors can join the festive *cinq-à-sept* (5pm-to-7pm) crowd over happy-hour drinks at stylish haunts before moving the party to underground clubs nearby.

Old Montréal is also a gateway to outdoor activities, with everything from picnicking along the waterfront to boat cruises on the St-Lawrence (and outdoor ice-skating for those who come in winter). Cyclists, joggers, in-line skaters and strollers can take a scenic trip along the Canal de Lachine, which goes for nearly 15km west to the edge of the Lac St-Louis. For more on Old Montréal's attractions, see p54.

>2 BASILIQUE NOTRE-DAME

COUNT YOUR BLESSINGS AMID THE BEAUTY OF QUÉBEC'S GRANDEST *ÉGLISE*

One of Montréal's most enduring symbols, this striking basilica occupies a site rich with three centuries of history. In order to create the neo-Gothic masterpiece, the Sulpicians commissioned James O'Donnell, a New York architect and Irish Protestant, to design what would be the largest church north of Mexico. Such was O'Donnell's dedication to the project that he converted to Catholicism so he could be buried in the basilica.

Opened in 1829, the basilica, which is loosely modeled on Ste-Chapelle in Paris, has a spectacular interior with a forest of ornate wood pillars and carvings made entirely by hand (and constructed without the aid of a single nail). Gilt stars shine from the ceiling vaults and the altar is backlit in electric blues. The massive Casavant organ with 5772 pipes is a thrill to hear, particularly at the famous Christmas concerts; the church bell, the Gros Bourdon, is the largest on the continent. Stained-glass windows depict scenes from Montréal's history rather than the usual biblical stories.

The Chapelle du Sacré Coeur (Sacred Heart Chapel) located behind the main hall is nicknamed the Wedding Chapel. It's so popular that couples might have to wait two years to tie the knot. The curious mix of styles emerged after a 1978 fire, when the chapel was rebuilt with a brass altar with abstract-modern motifs. For information on visiting the church, see p56.

>3 MUSÉE D'ARCHÉOLOGIE POINTE-À-CALLIÈRE

DELVE INTO THE EARLIEST DAYS OF MONTRÉAL

Built on the spot where European settlers set up their first camp in 1642, the Pointe-à-Callière Museum of Archaeology and History provides an excellent overview of Montréal's beginnings.

The largely subterranean museum houses a wide-ranging collection of artifacts spanning many centuries. Visitors descend in semidarkness to the archaeological crypt holding the remains of the city's ancient sewage and river system and the foundations of its first buildings and first public square. Excavations also reveal Canada's first Catholic cemetery (1634). Interactive exhibits throughout illustrate what life in the colony was like for residents in the 17th and 18th centuries.

An 18th-century market is re-created on Place Royale in summer, and the museum also hosts worthwhile temporary exhibitions. Plus, you can take a peak inside the Old Customs House (containing the museum's book and curio shop), reached by underground passage from the museum.

The lookout at the top of the tower in the new building provides an excellent view of the Old Port (pictured above).

For info on visiting the museum, see p58.

>4 PLATEAU DU MONT ROYAL

STROLL THE TREE-LINED STREETS OF MONTRÉAL'S MOST CHARMING NEIGHBORHOOD

One of Montréal's best-loved neighborhoods, the Plateau is packed with great restaurants and bars, picturesque boulevards, diverse residents (but stereotypically young and good looking) and a burgeoning art scene. Strolling through the pretty, tree-lined back streets reveals the Plateau in all its characteristic allure, with Victorian triplexes sporting ornate wrought-iron balconies, mansard roofs and winding exterior staircases, which become an essential social space in the summer.

Meanwhile, thoroughfares like blvd St-Laurent ('The Main'), rue St-Denis and av du Mont-Royal, have cafes, European-style brasseries and colorful shops selling everything from vintage clothing to avant-garde sculpture to gourmet ice cream. Although gentrification has arrived in full force to this once immigrant neighborhood, the Plateau still retains its bohemian vibe, and makes for some of the most rewarding exploring anywhere in Montréal. For more on the Plateau, see p78.

>5 PARC DU MONT-ROYAL

HEAD TO 'THE MOUNTAIN' FOR FRESH AIR, GREAT VIEWS AND IDYLLIC SCENERY

Montrealers are proud of their 'mountain,' so don't call it a hill – as Oscar Wilde did when he visited the city in the 1880s. The charming, leafy expanse of Mont Royal Park, which tops out at 201m, makes a magical setting for a range of activities, including jogging, cycling, picnicking, horseback riding and tossing around Frisbees. Winter brings skating, tobogganing, carriage rides through the snow and cross-country skiing.

The wooded slopes and grassy meadows have stunning views over the city, and there's even fine bird-watching in the park (keep an eye out for bird-feeders that have been set up along some walking trails).

The park was laid out in 1874 by Frederick Law Olmsted, the architect of New York's Central Park. Despite ravaging storms over the years (notably in 1998, when an ice storm destroyed thousands of trees), it remains the city's best and biggest park, spread over 100 hectares. In summer, don't miss the Sunday 'tam-tams' jam fest on the northeast side. For more details on the park, see p79.

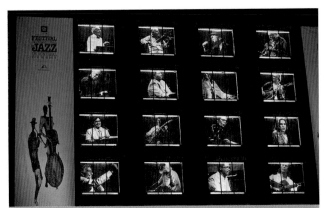

>6 LIVE MUSIC

FIND YOUR GROOVE IN THE CITY OF ENDLESS INVENTION

Sometimes it seems Montréal is all about the music. A friend to experimentation of all genres and styles, the city is home to more than 250 active bands, embracing anything and everything from electropop, hip-hop and glam rock to Celtic folk, indie punk and *yéyé* ('60s-style French pop) – not to mention roots, ambient, grunge and rockabilly. No matter what your weakness, you could spend all summer exploring Montréal's great soundtrack and still end up only scratching the surface.

There are dozens of large and medium-sized venues and theaters that host concerts. The best concert venue of all is downtown Montréal during the monster International Jazz Festival (Jazz Fest; see p26; pictured above) when it seems the whole city comes out to party.

Outside the frenetic festival weeks, the contemporary jazz scene bubbles away in a few hot spots like House of Jazz (p52) and Upstairs Jazz Bar & Grill (p53). Outside of jazz, those looking for the latest up-and-coming talent can head to small, intimate clubs in the Plateau (p78), Mile End (p92) and the Village (p70) – which is just the beginning of the great musical journey that awaits in Montréal.

>7 DINING

WITNESS (AND TASTE!) THE QUÉBÉCOIS CULINARY REVOLUTION IN ACTION

Boasting more than 5000 restaurants, Montréal is one of the great foodie destinations of the north. The dining scene is marked by dazzling variety and quality, and brash chefs who attack their creations with innovative gusto. Life in Montréal revolves around food, and it's as much about satisfying your sensual fantasies as it is about nourishment.

With so many incredible options, the hardest part is deciding where to begin. If time is limited, head straight to blvd St-Laurent, a street that encapsulates the city's gastronomic wealth. Here you'll find the atmospheric restaurants of Chinatown (p65), icons like Schwartz's smoked-meat emporium (pictured above; p86) and funky Plateau trendsetters like Au Pied de Cochon (p83). Just above the Plateau sits Mile End, home to stylish neighborhood bistros and Montréal's best bagels, while further north looms Little Italy with its old-world trattorias and market-fresh decadence at the sprawling Marché Jean Talon (p99). For finely crafted haute cuisine amid historic surroundings, book a table at L'Orignal (p64), Garde-Manger (p63) or at a growing number of innovative restaurants in Old Montréal (p63).

For more on the great culinary experience of Québec, see p128.

>8 PARC JEAN-DRAPEAU

PAY A VISIT TO THE INTRIGUING ISLANDS IN THE ST-LAWRENCE

Spreading across two islands in the St-Lawrence, the Parc Jean-Drapeau makes a splendid break from big-city bustle. This was the home of the highly successful 1967 World's Fair, and relics of its groundbreaking exhibitions still stand. The islands lie just one subway stop from Old Montréal (or a 20-minute bike ride) but seem a world removed from the busy streets across the river.

On Île Ste-Hélène walkways meander along the island through gardens and past evocative public art – like Alexander Calder's *L'Homme* (Humankind; p106) – with the Buckminster Fuller–designed Biosphère (pictured above; p106) a constant frame of reference. Here you can also join the mayhem at Montréal's favorite amusement park or dance beneath the summer sun at Piknic Électronik (p109), the long-running dance party that erupts every Sunday afternoon.

Neighboring Île Notre-Dame emerged in 10 months from the riverbed atop millions of tons of earth and rock excavated from the new métro created in 1967. Here you'll find canals and garden walkways, along with a Formula One racetrack, freely open to cyclists, joggers and in-line skaters. The island also has a large casino and even has its own lake (p108), a refreshing spot to cool off during hot summer days.

See p104 for more.

>9 MUSÉE DES BEAUX-ARTS

GAZE UPON MONTRÉAL'S MOST CELEBRATED MASTERPIECES

Montréal's Museum of Fine Arts, the oldest in the country and the city's largest, houses an impressive collection of artwork – over 35,000 pieces – spanning many centuries. The European masters are all on hand, including paintings by Rembrandt, Picasso and Matisse and sculptures by Moore, Giacometti and Calder. The museum's stellar attractions, however, are works by Canadian artists – with memorable portraits by Jean-Baptiste Roy-Audy, indigenous paintings by Paul Kane, wildly imaginative abstractions by Jean-Paul Riopelle and landscapes by the Group of Seven.

Two buildings house the museum's wide-ranging collection: the neoclassical Michal and Renata Hornstein Pavilion, and the ultra-modern Jean-Noël Desmarais Pavilion designed by Moishe Safdie. An underground tunnel links the two.

The latter plays host to works by European and Canadian masters but also ancient artifacts from Egypt, Greece, Rome and the Far East; Islamic art; and works from Africa and Oceania. The classical pavilion houses the Musée des Arts Décoratifs, with pieces from some of the world's most influential designers. The eclectic collection includes glass vases, Victorian chests, home appliances and an Inuit gallery as well as sections on industrial and graphic design.

For more details on visiting the museum, see p43.

>10 QUÉBEC CITY

DRINK IN THE BEAUTY OF CANADA'S OLDEST CITY

The crown jewel of French Canada, Québec City (p110) is one of the oldest European settlements in North America. Its picturesque Old Town is a Unesco World Heritage Site, a living museum of narrow cobbled streets lined with 17th- and 18th-century houses, with narrow church spires soaring overhead. There's more than a glimmer of Old Europe in its classic bistros and brasseries, sidewalk cafes and manicured parks and plazas.

Located on a strategic cliff above the St-Lawrence, its massive citadel bears testament to the crucial role this settlement played in the history of the New World. Indeed, history lurks around every corner of this atmospheric city, and its historical superlatives are many. This is, after all, home to the continent's first parish church, its first museum, first Anglican cathedral and first French-speaking university, among many other firsts. When you flip through the *Québec-Chronicle-Telegraph*, you're reading North America's oldest newspaper, and if you have to pay a visit to L'Hôtel Dieu de Québec, console yourself with the thought that it's the continent's oldest hospital.

What this historical onslaught adds up to is an aged capital that still carries the spirit of its days past, with twinges of romance, melancholy, eccentricity and intrigue lurking in its windswept lanes. This is also a city that goes to great lengths to attract (and amuse) visitors. Although busloads of tourists arrive during the summer, the buzz in the air and lively street life somehow counterbalance the mayhem of the masses. Musicians, acrobats and actors in period costume take to the streets and squares, while fantastic festivals fill the city with song.

Fall and spring bring beautiful colors, dramatically reduced prices and thinner crowds. And in the winter, Caribou, an alcoholic drink enjoyed by the early settlers, is sold everywhere to keep people warm and toasty. Even in the darkest and coldest months of January and February, Quebecers have found a way to have fun: throwing the annual Winter Carnival, arguably the biggest, most colorful and most successful winter festival around.

Once past Fairmont Le Château Frontenac (pictured right; p117), the most photographed hotel in the world, visitors find themselves

torn between the various neighborhoods' diverse charms. In Old Upper Town, the historical hub, there are some fine museums and restaurants among the *fleur-de-lis* T-shirt stores. Old Lower Town – at the base of the steep cliffs – is a labyrinth, where it's a pleasure to get lost among street performers and cozy inns before emerging on the north shore of the St-Lawrence.

One of the best ways to see these areas and to savor Québec's unique atmosphere is to grab a table at a sidewalk cafe and watch the lively street scene unfold.

HIGHLIGHTS

>11 FESTIVALS

JOIN THE REVELRY AT ONE OF QUÉBEC'S GRAND FÊTES

Famed for its unbridled spirit of *joie de vivre*, Montréal has a fantastic line-up of colorful fêtes spanning the calendar year. The city's best-known event is the riotous jazz festival, which erupts in late June each year, and turns the city into an enormous stage. No longer just about jazz, this is one of the world's biggies, with hundreds of top-name performers bringing reggae, rock, blues, world music – and even jazz – to audiophiles from across the globe. Québec City has its own musical mayhem that unfolds during its popular concert-packed Summer Festival.

Music is just one part – albeit an integral one – of celebrating *à la Québécois*. Other memorable festivals are dedicated to comedy, dance, art, theater, world cinema and even beer. Fireworks competitions fill the summer skies, while Montréal's Gay Pride brings hundreds of thousands of revelers to the city. Even in the dark of winter, the cities find cause for celebration, at Montréal's Snow Festival and Québec City's enormous Winter Carnival (pictured above). For the complete low-down on the city's annual events, see opposite.

> CALENDAR

Described by some as the city of festivals, Montréal has a packed calendar of lively fêtes, particularly during the summer, when entire blocks close to traffic, and stages appear for free concerts, improv and cinema. Québec City also has its celebrations, including a wild winter fest. As well as tourist office websites (see p158), good places to find out what's on include mags such as *Snap! Magazine* (www.snapme.ca), *Naked Eye* (www.nakedeyemag.com), free weeklies such as the *Mirror* (www.montrealmirror.com) and the French-only *Voir* (www.voir.ca) plus the English daily the *Montreal Gazette* (www.montrealgazette.com).

Montréal International Jazz Festival (p26)

JANUARY & FEBRUARY

La Fête des Neiges, Montréal

www.fetedesneiges.com; Île Ste-Hélène, Parc Jean-Drapeau

Montréal's Snow Festival features ice-sculpting contests, dog-sled races, snow games and costumed characters, such as mascot polar bear Boule de Neige. It's held over three consecutive weekends in late January and early February.

Winter Carnival, Québec City

www.carnaval.qc.ca

This famous annual event, held all over Québec City's Old Town, bills itself as the biggest winter carnival in the world. Between late January and mid-February, the Carnival features parades, ice sculptures, a snow slide, boat races, dances, music and lots of drinking. Plan early, as accommodations fill up quickly.

Montréal en Lumière

www.montrealhighlights.com

Created to help locals shake off the late-winter doldrums, the Montréal Highlights Festival is a kind of wintry Mardi Gras, held in February, with most events taking place downtown. There are classical music and dance performances, exhibitions, fireworks, celebrity chefs and innovative events, such as a 2.5km art gallery lining the Underground City.

A larger-than-life ice sculpture at Québec City's Winter Carnival

MARCH

Montréal Fashion Week

www.mfw.ca

This twice-yearly fashion event (March for the winter/fall collections and October for the spring/summer collections) is closed to the general public, but is worth noting for the excitement it generates around local fashion, and the festivities that spill over into local bars afterwards.

APRIL

Blue Metropolis – Montréal International Literary Festival

www.blue-met-bleu.com

Held in the first week of April, this festival brings together 200-plus writers from all over the globe for five days of literary events in English, French, Spanish and other languages.

BIENNALE DE MONTRÉAL

One of Montréal's most creative events showcases the best and the brashest on the Canadian art scene, including conferences and seminars on contemporary art. Expect interactive, cutting-edge multimedia pieces, often with opportunities for viewer participation. Upcoming dates are May of 2011. Visit www.biennalemontreal.org for more information.

MAY

Festival TransAmériques, Montréal

www.fta.qc.ca

Formerly known as *the* cutting-edge drama showcase *Festival de Théâtre des Amériques,* this festival casts a wide net, showcasing new and exciting drama, dance and performing art (with artists from around the globe). It runs from late May to early June in venues all over town.

JUNE

Montréal Beer Festival

www.festivalmondialbiere.qc.ca

Quaff brews from around the globe inside the old Windsor Station, at 1160 rue de la Gauchetière, Downtown. The five-day event starts in early June.

Tour de l'Île, Montréal

www.velo.qc.ca

Also known as the Montréal Bikefest, the Tour draws 30,000 enthusiasts for a 50km spin around the Island of Montréal, and a big party in the city afterwards. It's staged on the first Saturday in June.

Nuit Blanche sur Tableau Noir, Montréal

www.tableaunoir.com

Av du Mont-Royal becomes an artist's canvas on the second weekend in June as

CALENDAR

artists paint giant frescoes on the street. Music, various workshops, street food and children's activities add to the din.

St-Ambroise Montréal Fringe Festival

www.montrealfringe.ca

An off Broadway–style theater and repertory festival of new local and international talent, with dancing, music and the ever-popular drag races (as in drag-*queen* races). Held over 10 days in mid-June.

Fête Nationale du Québec, Québec City

www.fetenationale.qc.ca

Québec City parties hard on June 24, honoring John the Baptist, the patron saint of French Canadians. The day has evolved into a quasi-political event celebrating Québec culture. Major festivities on the Plains of Abraham start around 8pm, ending with a massive fireworks display.

JULY

Off-Festival de Jazz, Montréal

www.lofffestivaldejazz.com

The alternative jazz fest presents dozens of shows in several downtown venues to showcase young new talent. It's held over 10 days in late June and early July.

Montréal International Jazz Festival

Jazz Fest; www.montrealjazzfest.com

With over 400 concerts and nearly two million visitors every year, Montréal's best-known jamfest features a stellar line up of world music, folk and rock alongside jazz legends and upstarts. Hundreds of musicians hit the halls and outdoor stages, with plenty of free concerts over the two-week event held from late June to mid-July.

Loto-Québec International Fireworks Competition, Montréal

www.internationaldesfeuxloto -quebec.com

Thousands camp out on rooftops and on the Jacques-Cartier Bridge for this brilliant, dazzling pyrotechnics contest, accompanied by dramatic musical scores. The 10 shows last 30 minutes each and are held on Saturday nights and a few Wednesday nights from late June to the end of July.

Festival d'Été, Québec City

Summer Festival; www.infofestival.com

One of Canada's biggest events, this 11-day festival brings over 1.7 million music lovers to town. The city hosts some 300 concerts at performance halls, outdoor stages and on the street, with a line up of blues, reggae, rock, *chanson* (folk singing), pop, electronica and classical.

Festival International Nuits d'Afrique, Montréal

www.festivalnuitsdafrique.com

Celebrates the cultures of Africa and the Caribbean with more than 500 artists from

20-plus countries, with workshops, exotic cuisine and an African market. Held at Place Émilie-Gamelin and several clubs and halls for 10 days in mid-July.

Just for Laughs, Montréal

www.hahaha.com

This big comedy fest in the Quartier Latin draws dozens of well-known and up-and-coming performers to the two-week event running in mid-July. Past events have featured artists such as Whoopi Goldberg, Craig Ferguson, John Cleese and Margaret Cho.

Divers/Cité, Montréal

www.diverscite.org

Montréal's Gay Pride is *the* event on the Village calendar, drawing more than one million people. The streets around the Place Émilie-Gamelin pulse with dancing, art exhibits, concerts and parades. It is held over one week starting in late July.

Montréal International Dragon Boat Race

☎ 866-7001; www.montrealdragon boat.com

Rowing teams from all over the world compete in Chinese Dragon Boats on Île Notre-Dame, punctuated by entertainment and gastronomic events. Held over one weekend in late July.

Shakespeare in the Park, Montréal

www.shakespeareinthepark.ca

Families spread out on blankets for performances of the bard's plays at park stages around town on weekends, usually throughout July and August.

AUGUST & SEPTEMBER

Les FrancoFolies, Montréal

www.francofolies.com

The annual musical showcase of international French-language music and theater has today's biggest stars, and those on the rise, in over 200 shows and free outdoor presentations during 10 days in August.

Les FrancoFolies music festival, Montréal

Montréal World Film Festival

www.ffm-montreal.org

One of the most prestigious film events in Canada, attracts 400,000 visitors to screenings from 70 countries. It's held over 10 days in late August and early September.

OCTOBER

Festival du Nouveau Cinéma de Montréal

www.nouveaucinema.ca

This festival highlights who is up-and-coming in feature films, documentaries, experimental shorts, videos, narrative features and electronic art forms during 10 days in early October.

Black & Blue Festival

www.bbcm.org

One of the biggest gay events in the Village, with major dance parties, cultural and art shows as well as a megaparty in the Olympic Stadium, all in the second week of October.

Montréal Fashion Week

Spring/summer collections are shown in the second session of this twice-yearly event. See the listing under March (p25) for more information.

Biosphère (p106)

ITINERARIES

There's a fitting French verb for the ideal method of experiencing these two captivating cities: *flâner,* meaning to stroll. The Québécois are dedicated *flâneurs,* taking in the sights and sounds, dipping into shops and markets, leaving plenty of room for improvisation – perhaps a bite at that charming bistro that appears around the corner.

DAY ONE IN MONTRÉAL

Spend the day wandering the historic streets of Old Montréal (p54). Pay a visit to Basilique Notre-Dame (p56), learn about the city's history in the underground Musée d'Archéologie Pointe-à-Callière (p58), have lunch at Olive + Gourmando (p65), then explore the Old Port (p58). As afternoon nears, join the *cinq-à-sept* (5pm-to-7pm) crowd for outdoor drinks at Cafe des Éclusiers (p66). Later that night, enjoy a decadent meal at L'Orignal (p64).

DAY TWO IN MONTRÉAL

On day two take in the sights and sounds of downtown Montréal, starting at the Musée des Beaux-Arts (p43). Do a bit of window-shopping along rue Ste-Catherine, before heading to Chinatown (p65) for an authentic Cantonese feast. After lunch, take in the atmosphere of the Plateau du Mont Royal (p78), lingering along av du Mont-Royal or rue St-Denis, with their colorful stores and terrace cafes. Dine that evening at renowned Au Pied de Cochon (p83), followed by drinks at Plan B (p88).

DAY THREE IN MONTRÉAL

The third day, hire a bike for a tour of the city *à bicyclette* (p155). Pedal along the Canal de Lachine, stopping at the Marché Atwater (p49) for tasty, fresh picnic fare. Ride over to Parc Jean-Drapeau (p104) for a peaceful island spin, then head up to Parc du Mont-Royal (p79) for a splendid view over town. Afterwards, recharge at the Café Santropol (p83). In the afternoon, take in the old-world charms of Little Italy (p92) before heading down to Mile End (p92) for dinner and drinks along av Laurier. End the evening at Baldwin Barmacie (p102).

Left Rich colors emit warmth from an art shop window in rue St-Paul, Old Montréal

QUÉBEC CITY IN ONE DAY

Start your day at La Citadelle (p113). After that, wander through the Parc des Champs de Bataille (Battlefields Park; p115), a leafy park packed with historic sites. In the afternoon, head to the picturesque streets of the Old Upper Town, making sure to stop in at the Basilique-Cathédrale Notre-Dame-de-Québec (p112). In the evening, head down to Old Lower Town for a lavish meal at Laurie Raphaël (p119). Afterwards, catch a bit of québécois folk music at atmospheric Les Voûtes de Napoléon (p123).

RAINY DAY IN QUÉBEC CITY

Québec City is known for its frigid and often-drizzly weather. If you're caught in the rain or snow, make it a museum day. Start in the fascinating Musée de la Civilisation (p113), with outstanding exhibits covering the history of Québec. Follow with a bit of art appreciation at the stellar Musée National des Beaux-Arts (p115). If you're not stricken by museum fatigue, hit the Centre d'Interpretation de Place-Royale (p112); otherwise linger over a coffee and snack at Chez Temporel (p119). For dinner, have a long traditional meal at Aux Anciens Canadiens (p119). You'll feel cozy next to the fireplace, no matter how loud the wind howls outside.

Experience authentic québécois fare at Aux Anciens Canadiens (p119), Québec City

FORWARD PLANNING

Three to six months before you go If you're going to Jazz Fest or another big event, book tickets for shows. Scan www.admission.com for upcoming sports and entertainment events.

Two to three weeks before you go Book a table at one of Montréal's top-notch restaurants like Toqué! (p66). Take a browse through local websites like Midnight Poutine (www.midnightpoutine.com) and epicurean Eat Well Montréal (www.eatwellmontreal.com).

One week before you go Check the tourist-office website (www.tourisme-montreal.org) to see what art exhibitions are on when you're in town, and take a peek at Montreal Clubs (www.montreal-clubs.com) for parties and nightclub openings.

MONTRÉAL FOR FREE

There are lots of great ways to experience the city without spending a dime. Take a stroll along the Canal de Lachine. Head to the Sunday jamfest at Parc du Mont-Royal (p79). Climb to the top of Sailors' Memorial Clock Tower (p59) for a view over the waterfront. Visit the Musée d'Art Contemporain (p42) on Wednesday night when it's free, or the Musée des Beaux-Arts (p43), which is always free (special exhibits charge, but are also free on Wednesday nights). Better yet, schedule your visit around Montréal Museums day, when 30 museums are free (www.museesmontreal.org), usually in late May. Many festivals, including Jazz Fest (p26) host free concerts. Arguably, one of Montréal's best forms of entertainment – people-watching – costs little more than the price of a cup of coffee at a sidewalk cafe in the Plateau (p78).

Église Notre-Dame-des-Victoires (p112), Québec City

NEIGHBORHOODS

Montréal has a complicated soul. Elements of Europe and North America, along with an alluring spirit of bohemianism all play a role in shaping the elusive identity of La Belle Ville.

This is a city of grand cathedrals, old-world markets and cobblestone streets still lined with 17th-century stone buildings. European virtues aside, Montréal retains her North American roots – from the love of a good sports bar to adulation of the latest trends emerging from Canada's southern neighbor. Add to this the fascinating blend of anglophones and francophones, plus the surprising diversity of Montréal's newest arrivistes, and the city begins to reveal herself in all her dynamic beauty.

Each neighborhood of Montréal presents a distinct world, complete with its own color, character and energy (not to mention language!). For the *flâneur* (wanderer), Montréal offers boundless intrigue in the form of avant-garde art galleries, kitsch-loving boutiques, bohemian-style jazz bars and flower-filled parks for taking a respite from the streets.

On the edge of the St-Lawrence, Old Montréal is the city's birthplace, with picturesque squares and grand old-world architecture. The buzz of Downtown lies just west, with bustling streets and a sprinkling of top-notch museums and restaurants. North of Old Montréal lies the pint-sized but colorful Chinatown, while the lively cafes and low-key bars of the Quartier Latin and the adjoining Village (a major icon for gay travelers) stretch further east. Further north is the Plateau du Mont Royal, a once-immigrant neighborhood that houses the best assortment of dining and nightlife. Just up from the Plateau are Mile End and Outremont, two leafy neighborhoods with upscale boutiques and restaurants; nearby, Little Italy offers a taste of old-world street life and well-loved cafes.

260km northeast of Montréal, Québec City boasts a dramatic setting on the bluffs of the St-Lawrence, complete with a jewel-box Old Town lined with historic buildings and European-style brasseries. Québec City is also the capital and power center of the province.

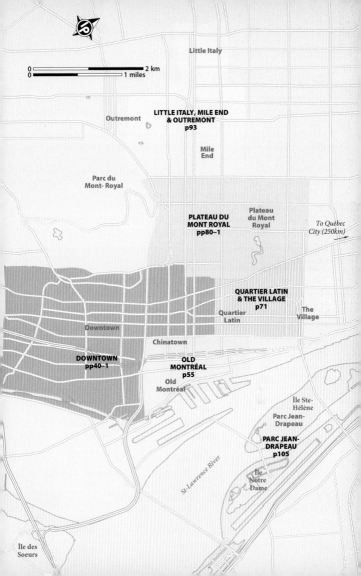

Little Italy

LITTLE ITALY, MILE END & OUTREMONT
p93

Outremont

Mile
End

Parc du
Mont- Royal

**PLATEAU DU
MONT ROYAL**
pp80–1

Plateau
du Mont
Royal

*To Québec
City (250km)*

**QUARTIER LATIN
& THE VILLAGE**
p71

Quartier
Latin

The
Village

Downtown

Chinatown

DOWNTOWN
pp40–1

**OLD
MONTRÉAL**
p55

Old
Montréal

Île Ste-
Hélène
Parc Jean-
Drapeau

**PARC JEAN-
DRAPEAU**
p105

St-Lawrence River

Île
Notre
Dame

Île des
Soeurs

0 _____ 2 km
0 _____ 1 miles

>DOWNTOWN

Downtown Montréal hums with energy. Its mix of wide boulevards, glass skyscrapers and shopping galleries give the area a decidedly North American flavor, while numerous green spaces, eye-catching heritage buildings and 19th-century churches add a more European character to the bustling city streets. On weekdays, Downtown draws an equally diverse crowd, from well-dressed businesspeople power-lunching at high-end restaurants to backpack-toting students who flood the district each day en route to McGill or Concordia.

Downtown is also home to some of Montréal's best museums, and is a popular place with the after-work crowd for a wide variety of urban distractions. A few key destinations in the area include the long thoroughfare of rue Ste-Catherine, which is packed with boutiques and

DOWNTOWN

◎ SEE
Cathédrale Marie-Reine-
  du-Monde 1 E4
Centre Canadien
  d'Architecture 2 C3
Galeries d'Art Contemporain
  du Belgo 3 G3
McGill University 4 F2
Montréal Planetarium ..5 E5
Musée d'Art
  Contemporain 6 G3
Musée des Beaux-Arts ..7 D2
Musée McCord 8 F3
Parisian Laundry 9 A4

🏃 DO
Atrium Le 1000 ....10 F4
H2O Adventures 11 A6
My Bicyclette 12 A6

🛍 SHOP
Boutique Eva B 13 H3
Chapters Bookstore 14 E3

Holt Renfrew 15 E2
Hudson Bay
  Company 16 F3
Les Antiquités Grand
  Central 17 B5
Ogilvy 18 E3
Place Ville-Marie 19 F4

🍴 EAT
Amelio's 20 G2
Café Ferreira 21 E3
Joe Beef..................(see 24)
Le Paris 22 C3
Le Taj 23 E3
Liverpool House 24 B5
Lola Rosa 25 F2
M:Brgr 26 E3
Marché Atwater 27 A5
Phaya Thai 28 D3
Première Moisson 29 A5
Queue de Cheval 30 E4
Restaurant Globe 31 H2
Reuben's 32 E3

🍸 DRINK
Brutopia 33 D3
Burgundy Lion 34 B5
Grumpy's Bar 35 D3
Koko 36 G2
Mad Hatter Saloon 37 D3
Nyk's Map...............(see 3)
Pub Ste-Élisabeth 38 H3
Sir Winston Churchill
  Pub 39 D3

⭐ PLAY
Club 737 ....40 F4
Comedyworks 41 D3
Cubano's Club 42 G3
Foufounes Electriques .43 H3
House of Jazz 44 F3
L'Opéra de Montréal ...45 G3
Orchestre Symphonique
  de Montréal ....(see 45)
SAT........................46 H3
Upstairs Jazz Bar & Grill 47 D3

Please see over for map

shopping galleries (particularly between rue Crescent and rue University, E3). Meanwhile, rue Crescent and rue Bishop (D3) are the traditional anglophone centers of nightlife with an array of bars and restaurants. Rue Sherbrooke Ouest features upscale shops and turn-of-the-century residences with a pronounced English flavor.

◉ SEE

◉ CATHÉDRALE MARIE-REINE-DU-MONDE

☎ 514-866-1661; 1045 rue de la Cathédrale; ☼ 7:30am-6pm; Ⓜ Bonaventure

The Cathedral of Mary Queen of the World (completed in 1894) is a smaller but still magnificent version of St Peter's Basilica in Rome. The architects scaled it down to one-quarter size, mindful of the structural risks of Montréal's severe winters.

◉ CENTRE CANADIEN D'ARCHITECTURE

☎ 514-939-7026; www.cca.qc.ca; 1920 rue Baile; admission $10; ☼ 11am-6pm Wed & Fri-Sun, to 9pm Thu; Ⓜ Guy-Concordia

A must for architecture fans, this center is equal parts museum and research institute. The building incorporates the Shaughnessy House, a 19th-century gray limestone treasure, with a lovely assortment of period furnishings. The Centre hosts architecturally related exhibitions, and there's a sculpture garden overlooking southern Montréal.

◉ GALERIES D'ART CONTEMPORAIN DU BELGO

372 rue Ste-Catherine Ouest; Ⓜ Place-d'Armes

Over a decade ago the Belgo building was a run-down haven for struggling artists. It quickly earned a reputation as one of Montréal's most important

---

SACRED PROFANITY

The French spoken in Québec has a character all its own and cursing is no exception. Here, swear words center on the objects used in church services, a legacy of the church's centuries-long dominance. The words are untranslatable, but where a displeased English speaker might yell 'fuck', a Quebecer will unleash *tabarnac* (from tabernacle). Instead of 'oh, shit!', a Quebecer will cry *sacrament!* (from sacrament). And if you've really messed up, just pray you're never on the receiving end of a combo like *'hostie de câlisse de tabarnac!'* (rough translation: 'host in the chalice in the tabernacle!').

Oddly enough, *fucké*, an adaptation of the English, is mild enough for prime time and means 'broken' or 'crazy'.

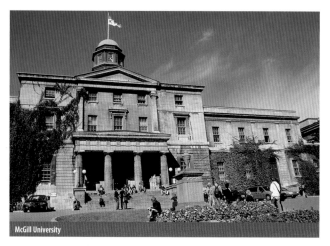

McGill University

exhibition spaces, with galleries, dance and photography studios. Designers, art dealers and architects now make up three-quarters of the tenancy. Take the elevator up to the 5th floor and conduct an art walking tour down to street level.

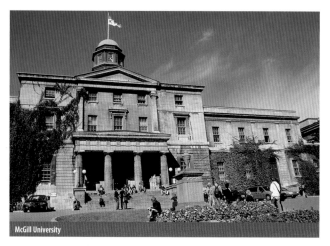 MCGILL UNIVERSITY

☎ 514-398-4455; www.mcgill.ca; 845 rue Sherbrooke Ouest; Ⓜ McGill
Founded in 1828 by James McGill, a rich Scottish fur trader, McGill is one of Canada's most prestigious universities. The leafy campus with its Victorian buildings is a pretty place for a stroll or a picnic.

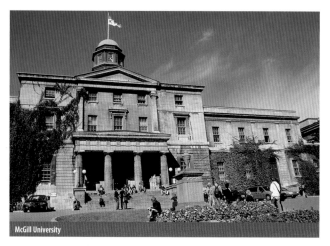 MONTRÉAL PLANETARIUM

☎ 514-872-4530; www.planetarium .montreal.qc.ca; 1000 rue St-Jacques; admission $8; Ⓜ Bonaventure
This 20m-high dome opens a window on the universe during narrated 50-minute shows, running alternately in French and English. Call for the current schedule.

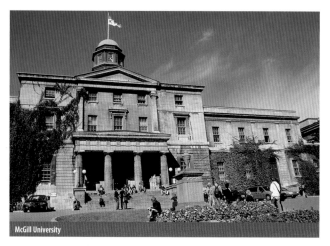 MUSÉE D'ART CONTEMPORAIN

☎ 514-847-6226; www.macm.org; 185 rue Ste-Catherine Ouest, Place des Arts; admission $8; 🕑 11am-6pm Tue & Thu-Sun, to 9pm Wed; Ⓜ Place-des-Arts
Canada's major showcase of contemporary art has eight galleries

divided between past greats (since 1939) and current developments. A weighty collection of 6000 permanent works includes Québec legends Marc-Aurèle Fortin, Jean-Paul Riopelle, Paul-Émile Borduas and Geneviève Cadieux.

MUSÉE DES BEAUX-ARTS
☎ 514-285-2000; www.mmfa.qc.ca; 1380 rue Sherbrooke Ouest; permanent collection free, special exhibits admission $15; ⏲ 11am-5pm Sat-Tue, Thu & Fri, to 9pm Wed; Ⓜ Guy-Concordia
Montréal's Museum of Fine Arts, founded in 1860, was one of the first museums in North America to amass such a large collection. More than 2000 years of art history is on display through painting,

IRISH IN MONTRÉAL
The Irish have been streaming into Montréal since the founding of New France, but they came in floods between 1815 and 1860, driven from Ireland by the potato famine. Catholic, like the French settlers, the Irish easily assimilated into québécois society. Today a phenomenal 45% of Quebecers have Irish ancestry somewhere in their family tree, though many of them don't even know it. In Montréal, most of these immigrants settled in Griffintown, then an industrial hub near the Canal de Lachine. A St Patrick's Day parade was first held in the city in 1824, and has run every year since; it's now one of the city's biggest events.

sculpture, decorative art, furniture, prints, drawings and photographs. For more information, see p19.

MUSÉE MCCORD
☎ 514-398-7100; www.mccord -museum.qc.ca; 690 rue Sherbrooke Ouest; admission $13; ⏲ 10am-6pm Tue-Fri, to 5pm Sat & Sun; Ⓜ McGill
This highly recommended museum houses over a million artifacts and documents illustrating Canada's social, cultural and archaeological history from the 18th century to present day.

PARISIAN LAUNDRY
☎ 514-989-1056; www.parisianlaundry .com; 3550 rue St-Antoine Ouest; ⏲ noon-5pm Tue-Sat; Ⓜ Lionel-Groulx
A former industrial laundry turned monster gallery, this 15,000-sq-ft space hosts an excellent line up of large-format contemporary art. It also holds occasional artists' talks and lectures.

🏃 DO
🏃 ATRIUM LE 1000 *Ice-skating*
☎ 514-395-0555; www.le1000.com; 1000 rue de la Gauchetière Ouest; admission $6, skate rental $5.50; Ⓜ Bonaventure
Enjoy year-round indoor ice-skating at this excellent glass-domed rink near Gare Central. Call for operating hours as the schedule changes frequently.

Kayaking fun with H2O Adventures

⚡ H2O ADVENTURES
Kayak Hire
☎ 514-998-6252; www.aventuresh2o
.com; Canal de Lachine; kayak/pedal
boat per hr $15/10; ⏲ 9am-9pm;
Ⓜ Charlevoix

On the canal's south bank near
Marché Atwater, H2O Adventures
offers kayak and pedal boat rent-
als as well as two-hour kayaking
courses ($39 to $45).

⚡ MY BICYCLETTE *Bicycle Hire*
☎ 514-998-6252; Canal de Lachine; bike
per hr/day $10/30; ⏲ 10am-7pm mid-
May–mid-Oct; Ⓜ Charlevoix

Across the canal from the Marché
Atwater, this outfit can get you
fully equipped (24-speed hybrids,
fat-tire cruisers, kids' bikes) for a
tranquil ride along the Canal de
Lachine.

🛍 SHOP
🏷 BOUTIQUE EVA B *Fashion*
☎ 514-849-8246; 2013 blvd St-Laurent;
⏲ 10am-7pm or later Mon-Sat, noon-
5pm Sun; Ⓜ St-Laurent

This boutique is a riot of recycled
women's clothing, retro gear and
new street wear. You'll find 1950s
bowling shoes, feather boas and

much more in this theatrical little store.

📖 CHAPTERS BOOKSTORE
Books, Music

☎ 514-849-8825; 1171 rue Ste-Catherine Ouest; 🕙 9am-10pm; Ⓜ Peel

Peruse three huge floors of English and French books, and a fantastic choice of travel-related items in the sunken floor at the back. There's a coffee bar and internet cafe on the 2nd floor.

📖 HOLT RENFREW
Department Store

☎ 514-842-5111; 1300 rue Sherbrooke Ouest; Ⓜ Peel

This Montréal institution is a godsend for label-conscious, cashed-up professionals and upscale shoppers. There's also an attractive on-site cafe.

📖 HUDSON BAY COMPANY
Department Store

☎ 514-281-4422; 585 rue Ste-Catherine Ouest; Ⓜ McGill

La Baie, as it's called in French, found fame three centuries ago

---

ANTIQUE ALLEY

Dozens of antique shops jostle for business on Antique Alley (C5), the stretch of rue Notre-Dame Ouest in the southwest part of Downtown between av Atwater and rue Guy.

---

for its striped wool blankets. Today this famous department store stocks just about everything, including cut-price garments on the 8th floor.

📖 LES ANTIQUITÉS GRAND CENTRAL *Antiques*

☎ 514-935-1467; 2448 rue Notre-Dame Ouest; 🕙 9am-6pm Mon-Sat; Ⓜ Lionel-Groulx

The most elegant store on Antique Alley (see the boxed text, left) is a pleasure to visit for its English and Continental furniture, lighting and decorative objects from the 18th and 19th centuries.

📖 OGILVY *Department Store*
☎ 514-842-7711; 1307 rue Ste-Catherine Ouest; Ⓜ Peel

Once a Victorian-era department store, Ogilvy has transformed itself into a collection of high-profile boutiques. Its front window displays mechanical toys that are a Montréal fixture at Christmas.

📖 PLACE VILLE-MARIE
Shopping Mall

☎ 514-861-9393; cnr av McGill College & rue Cathcart; Ⓜ Bonaventure

Established in the late 1950s, Montréal's first shopping complex marked the start of the underground city (see the boxed text, p46). It now hosts 80 boutiques, restaurants and service stores.

NEIGHBOURHOODS

DOWNTOWN

NEIGHBORHOODS

DOWNTOWN

THE UNDERGROUND CITY

'Underground city' is a bit of a misnomer. There are no subterranean skyscrapers or roads, just an extensive network of shops, restaurants, cinemas and exhibition halls — all linked by brightly lit, well-ventilated corridors (some 29km in all); trickling fountains help maintain humidity and the temperature hovers around 68°F (20°C). Add the métro and you've got a self-contained world, shielded from the subarctic temperatures. In the middle of winter, some particularly well-placed residents could go to work, do their grocery shopping, see a movie and take in a performance at Place des Arts and never need more than a T-shirt.

🍴 EAT

🍴 AMELIO'S *Italian* $$
☎ 514-845-8396; 201 rue Milton; mains $7-20; 🕑 11:30am-9pm Mon-Fri, from 4pm Sat & Sun; Ⓜ Place-des-Arts

Smack in the middle of the McGill student ghetto, this longtime favorite has fed generations of students with its satisfying portions of pizza and pasta. Pizzas boast crispy crusts and come heaped with toppings.

🍴 CAFÉ FERREIRA
Portuguese $$$
☎ 514-848-0988; 1446 rue Peel; mains $26-40; Ⓜ Peel

This warm and inviting restaurant serves some of Montréal's best Portuguese fare. The *cataplana* (bouillabaisse-style seafood stew) is magnificent, and meat lovers can feast on rack of lamb or spice-rubbed Angus rib-eye steak.

🍴 JOE BEEF *Québécois* $$$
☎ 514-935-6504; 2491 rue Notre-Dame Ouest; mains $22-35; Ⓜ Lionel-Groulx

In the heart of the Little Burgundy neighborhood, Joe Beef is the current darling of food critics for its unfussy, market-fresh fare. The rustic, country-kitsch setting is a great spot to linger over fresh oysters, tender Wagyu beef, fresh fish and a changing selection of hearty québécois dishes.

🍴 LE PARIS *French* $$
☎ 514-937-4898; 1812 rue Ste-Catherine Ouest; mains $16-30; 🕑 noon-3pm & 5:30-10:30pm Mon-Sat, 5:30-10:30pm Sun; Ⓜ Guy-Concordia

This casual neighborhood bistro opened in 1956 and still has a loyal following. The menu features no-frills French food – like duck confit and much-touted *branade de morue* (salt cod with cream and garlic).

🍴 LE TAJ *Indian* $$
☎ 514-845-9015; 2077 rue Stanley; mains $15-22; Ⓜ Peel

Le Taj prepares some of Downtown's best Indian food. It's

Frédéric Morin

One of the chef-owners of Joe Beef, which has garnered much attention for its exquisite québécois comfort fare

What keeps you in Montréal? It's cool to be in such a culturally rich place – growing up, your best friends are Italian and Lebanese, there's a Jewish neighborhood up the street, and you're the only québécois kid on your block. You move between French and English – not just linguistically, but culturally. I like that quote by the PM during the independence drive: 'We're all ethnics here; it just depends on your date of arrival.' **What are your favorite dishes?** I really love beef – a braised meat in winter, a thick steak in the summer. Sometimes I crave oysters and get the urge for greens. And I love Dover sole. **What's with the new garden you've created?** I get things for the restaurant in there – but most of my greens are from the Atwater market (p49). I do the garden for me. I love working in there. It's my happy place. **Describe the restaurant scene here** I love Paris and New York, but they're competitive. Cooks in restaurants here are friends. Maybe it's this laid-back city – the Canal de Lachine, the parks…

particularly popular for its lunchtime buffet ($13), featuring tandoori chicken, vegetable korma and tender lamb, along with steaming naan and many other temptations.

🍴 LIVERPOOL HOUSE
Québécois $$
☎ 514-313-6049; 2501 rue Notre-Dame Ouest; mains $18-26; Ⓜ Lionel-Groulx
From the same anti-establishment chefs that launched Joe Beef next door, this charming little eatery serves from an ever-changing menu of fresh bistro fare. If you can't score a table, try next door at McKiernan's, also part of the Joe Beef group.

🍴 LOLA ROSA *Vegetarian* $$
☎ 514-287-9337; 545 rue Milton; mains $12-24; Ⓨ 11:30am-9:30pm; Ⓜ McGill
On a leafy street near McGill, this charming and low-key cafe prepares delicious vegetarian food. A chalkboard menu displays daily specials, with fresh salads, juices, desserts and decent coffee on hand.

🍴 M:BRGR *Hamburgers* $$
☎ 514-906-2747; 2025 rue Drummond; burgers $9-15; Ⓨ 11:30am-11pm Mon-Sat, noon-9pm Sun; Ⓜ Peel
Bringing a gourmet touch to the humble hamburger, this stylish place serves juicy patties that can be dressed with smoked gouda, apple-smoked bacon as well

Marché Atwater

as other high-end toppings. To complete your experience here, add in sweet-potato fries and a thick milkshake – or better yet, a cocktail.

🍴 MARCHÉ ATWATER
Market $

☎ 514-937-7754; 138 av Atwater; ⌚ 7am-6pm Mon-Wed, to 8pm Thu & Fri, to 5pm Sat & Sun; Ⓜ Lionel-Groulx
This fantastic market has a mouth-watering assortment of fresh produce from local farms, excellent wines, crusty breads, fine cheeses and other delectable fare. And the nearby Canal de Lachine makes a great spot for a picnic. The excellent Première Moisson is a popular cafe and bakery. It's all housed in a 1933 brick hall, topped with a clock tower.

🍴 PHAYA THAI *Thai* $$
☎ 514-933-9949; 1235 rue Guy; mains $12-18; Ⓜ Guy-Concordia
Just off the beaten path, this casual little Thai restaurant serves good, fresh-tasting curries, satisfying duck and seafood plates and plenty of other delicacies from the east.

🍴 QUEUE DE CHEVAL
Steakhouse $$$

☎ 514-390-0090; 1221 blvd René-Lévesque Ouest; mains $28-41; ⌚ 11:30am-2:30pm Mon-Fri,

POUTINE
For the traditional taste of Québec order a *poutine* (fries smothered in cheese curds and gravy). Varieties include 'all dress' (sautéed mushrooms and bell pepper), 'richie boy' (ground beef), Italian (beef and spaghetti sauce), barbecue or even smoked meat. The idea is to eat up quickly since the curds can quickly turn the fries to mush.

5:30-10:30pm Sun-Wed, 5:30-11:30pm Thu-Sat; Ⓜ Lucien-L'Allier
One of the city's best steak-houses, Queue de Cheval grills up juicy cuts of prime beef that is dry-aged on the premises. Order from a dozen varieties of steaks and then watch the grilling pyrotechnics unfold in the open kitchen. Reservations recommended.

🍴 RESTAURANT GLOBE
International $$$

☎ 514-284-3823; 3455 blvd St-Laurent; mains $24-38; ⌚ 6-11pm Sun-Wed, to midnight Thu-Sat; Ⓜ St-Laurent, then 🚌 55
This stylish see-and-be-seen place features an imaginative menu combining high- and low-brow ingredients to create a decadent kind of comfort food (lobster mac'n'cheese, calamari stuffed with goat cheese and chorizo).

NEIGHBORHOODS

DOWNTOWN

REUBEN'S *Smoked Meat* $
☎ 514-866-1029; 1116 rue Ste-Catherine Ouest; mains $8-15; ⏱ 6:30am-midnight Mon-Wed, 6:30am-1:30am Thu & Fri, 8am-1:30am Sat, 8am-midnight Sun; Ⓜ Peel
Towering smoked-meat sandwiches served with big-cut fries are slammed down in booths and along the long counter that seems perennially crowded.

DRINK

BRUTOPIA *Pub*
☎ 514-393-9277; 1219 rue Crescent; ⏱ 3:30pm-3am Sun-Fri, noon-3am Sat; Ⓜ Guy-Concordia
Brutopia has eight varieties of suds on tap including honey beer, nut brown and the more challenging raspberry blonde. The brick walls and wood paneling are conducive to chats among this relaxed student crowd.

BURGUNDY LION
Pub, Restaurant
☎ 934-0888; 2496 rue de Notre-Dame Ouest; ⏱ 11:30am-3am Mon-Sat, from 10am Sun; Ⓜ Lionel-Groulx
This trendy take on the English pub, features British pub fare, beers and whiskeys galore, and an attitude-free vibe where everyone (and their parents) feels welcome to drink, eat and be merry. Tip your cap to Queen Elizabeth,

whose portrait adorns the bathroom door.

GRUMPY'S BAR *Pub*
☎ 514-866-9010; 1242 rue Bishop; ⏱ noon-3am; Ⓜ Guy-Concordia
This unassuming basement bar is a former stomping ground of Anglo intellectuals from an era gone by. Wednesdays are open-mic nights with comedy and spoken word, and most nights feature live music. Thursday nights are legendary, with acoustic bluegrass jam sessions.

KOKO *Restaurant, Bar*
☎ 514-657-5656; 8 rue Sherbrooke Ouest; ⏱ 11am-3pm Mon-Fri, 6-10pm Sun-Thu, 6-11pm Fri & Sat, bar open to 3am Fri & Sat; Ⓜ St-Laurent
The specialty cocktails and luxe surroundings of this loungey restaurant inside the Opus Hotel attract jetsetters and the city's fashion crowd. DJs mix house music on weekends and there's a massive outdoor terrace.

MAD HATTER SALOON *Bar*
☎ 514-987-9988; 1220 rue Crescent; ⏱ 11am-3am; Ⓜ Guy-Concordia
With happy-hour specials and a kooky, anything-goes feel, this longtime rue Crescent tavern has gathered the Concordia and McGill flock for years. The 2nd-floor terrace is a fine spot to unwind in the summertime.

DOWNTOWN

🍸 NYK'S MAP *Pub*
☎ 514-866-1787; 1250 rue de Bleury;
🕐 11am-3am Mon-Fri, from 4pm Sat;
Ⓜ Place-des-Arts

Its artsy-chic vibe makes this warm bistro pub the preferred lunch and after-work spot of Plateau cool kids who happen to work in downtown offices.

🍸 PUB STE-ÉLISABETH *Pub*
☎ 514-286-4302; 1412 rue Ste-Élisabeth;
🕐 3pm-3am; Ⓜ Berri-UQAM

Tucked off a side street, this little pub is revered by Montrealers for its vine-covered courtyard and impressive drink menu, which includes a fantastic array of beers on tap.

🍸 SIR WINSTON CHURCHILL PUB *Pub*
☎ 514-288-3814; 1459 rue Crescent;
🕐 11:30-3am; Ⓜ Guy-Concordia

Winnie's cavernous, split-level pub brings in a steady crowd of tourists, students and an older Anglo crowd. The draw: multiple bars, pool tables, pulsating music and meals served all day.

⭐ PLAY

☆ CLUB 737 *Club*
☎ 514-397-0737; 1 pl Ville-Marie;
🕐 5pm-3am; Ⓜ McGill

Try predinner drinks with the glam set on the 43rd floor – the romantic skyline never disappoints. Serious cruising goes on among the office crowd of 30-somethings.

☆ COMEDYWORKS
Comedy
☎ 514-398-9661; 1238 rue Bishop;
🕐 8pm-3am Mon-Sat; Ⓜ Guy-Concordia

This intimate comedy club is a fun place to catch emerging and established talent. Mondays are

---

POLICING THE LANGUAGE

Québec's French Language Charter, the (in)famous Bill 101, asserts the primacy of French on public signs across the province. Stop signs in Québec read 'ARRÊT' (even in France, the red hexagonal signs read 'STOP'), and English is allowed on signage provided it's no more than half the size of the French lettering. Perhaps most comical of all is the acronym PFK (Poulet Frit Kentucky) for the well-known fast-food chain – even communist China still allows signs for KFC (Kentucky Fried Chicken).

The law is vigorously enforced by language police who roam the province with tape measures and hand out fines if a door says 'Push' more prominently than '*Poussez*'. These days, most Quebecers take it all in their stride, and the comical language tussles between businesses and the language police have all but disappeared.

NEIGHBORHOODS

DOWNTOWN

open-mic; Tuesdays and Wednesdays noted improv troupe On the Spot Players take the stage. Reservations required.

 CUBANO'S CLUB *Club*
☎ 514-878-9009; 1186 rue Crescent; ☼ 10pm-3am; Ⓜ Place-des-Arts
This undisputed hub of Salsa, Afro-Cuban and Latin jazz is a great place to learn some new moves (dance classes are offered during the day). Big Cuban orchestras and mambo competitions take place during Jazz Fest (p26).

FOUFOUNES ELECTRIQUES *Club*
☎ 514-844-5539; 87 rue Ste-Catherine Est; ☼ 3pm-3am; Ⓜ St-Laurent
A one-time bastion of the alterna-freak, this cavernous quintessential punk venue still hosts edgy bands and uncommon events. On weekends the student-grunge crowd plays pool and quaffs brews with electro kids.

HOUSE OF JAZZ *Jazz*
☎ 514-842-8656; 2060 rue Aylmer; general admission $5; ☼ 11:30am-12:30am Mon-Wed, to 2:30am Thu & Fri, 6pm-2:30am Sat & Sun; Ⓜ McGill
This mainstream-but-excellent jazz club and restaurant serves up Southern-style cuisine and live jazz daily.

L'OPERA DE MONTRÉAL
Opera
☎ 514-985-2258; Place des Arts; tickets $50-140; ☼ box office 9am-5pm Mon-Fri; Ⓜ Place-des-Arts
Holds lavish stage productions that feature big names from Québec and around the world. Translations (French or English) run on a video screen above the stage.

ORCHESTRE SYMPHONIQUE DE MONTRÉAL
Classical Music
☎ 514-842-9951; Place des Arts, 260 blvd de Maisonneuve Ouest, Ⓜ Place-des-Arts

House of Jazz

This internationally renowned orchestra plays to packed audiences in its Place-des-Arts home. Its Christmas performance of the *Nutcracker* is legendary.

⭐ SAT *Club, Art Space*
☎ 514-844-2033; 1195 blvd St-Laurent;
Ⓜ St-Laurent

La Societé des Arts Technologiques (SAT) is a slick warehouse that promotes partying as much as digital art. DJs and performance artists push the envelope, while cult party brands like NEON host fêtes here.

⭐ UPSTAIRS JAZZ BAR & GRILL *Jazz*
☎ 514-931-6808; 1254 rue Mackay;
⌚ 5:30pm-2am, music from 8:30pm;
Ⓜ Guy-Concordia

This slick downtown bar hosts quality jazz and blues acts nightly, both local and touring talent. The walled terrace behind the bar is enchanting at sunset, and the dinner menu features inventive salads, plus grilled meats and seafood.

>OLD MONTRÉAL

Most visitors to the city begin their trip in Vieux-Montréal, drawn by its imposing churches, photogenic streets and fascinating museums relating the early days of French and British settlement in Canada. Ville Marie, the settlement that was to become Montréal, has gone through numerous incarnations, from hub of the fur trade to financial giant of Canada to kitschy tourist trap. In more recent days, it's become a trendy destination in its own right, with a crop of boutique hotels, award-winning restaurants and converted lofts attracting a younger, savvier crowd than in decades past.

A few focal points include Place Jacques-Cartier (D2), mecca of performance artists and eateries; and Place d'Armes (C2), home of the imposing Basilique Notre-Dame. Rue St-Paul (B3) teems with art galleries, shops and eateries. On the bank of the St-Lawrence, the broad concourse of the Old Port is lined with green parkland and cafes along rue de la Commune (D3).

OLD MONTRÉAL

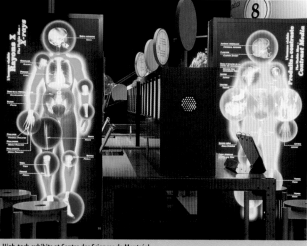 SEE

BASILIQUE NOTRE-DAME

☎ 514-842-2925; 110 rue Notre-Dame Ouest; admission $5; ◔ 7am-4:30pm Mon-Sat, 8am-4pm Sun, extended in summer, tours hourly Jul-Sep; Ⓜ Place-d'Armes

The grand dame of Montréal's ecclesiastical treasures, this basilica is a must-see when exploring the city. The looming neo-Gothic church can hold up to 3000 worshippers and houses a collection of finely crafted artworks, including an elaborately carved altarpiece, vibrant stained-glass windows and an intricate pulpit.

See p12 for more.

An evening **sound and light display** (admission $10; ◔ 6:30pm Tue-Thu, 6:30pm & 8:30pm Fri, 7pm & 8:30pm Sat) uses cutting-edge technology to tell the story of the church and the city.

CENTRE DES SCIENCES DE MONTRÉAL

☎ 514-496-4724; www.centredessciences deMontréal.com; admission $12-23; ◔ 9am-4pm Mon-Thu, 10am-9pm Fri & Sat, 10am-5pm Sun

This sleek science center on the waterfront houses virtual and in-

High-tech exhibits at Centre des Sciences de Montréal

teractive games and technology exhibits. Admission price varies depending on which combinations of films and/or exhibits you want to take in. The center includes an IMAX cinema that shows vivid nature and science films.

◎ CENTRE D'HISTOIRE DE MONTRÉAL

☎ 514-872-3207; 335 Place d'Youville; admission $6; ◷ 10am-5pm Tue-Sun; Ⓜ Square-Victoria

This small museum puts a human spin on city history in engaging multimedia exhibits. You can listen to the tales of real people while sitting in a period kitchen or travel back in time while watching archival footage from the '40s and '60s. For sweeping views, head to the rooftop.

◎ CHAPELLE NOTRE-DAME-DE-BONSECOURS

☎ 514-282-8670; www.marguerite -bourgeoys.com; 400 rue St-Paul Est; chapel free, museum admission $8; ◷ 10am-5:30pm Tue-Sun May-Oct, 11am-3:30pm Tue-Sun Nov–mid-Jan & March-April; Ⓜ Champ-de-Mars

This chapel is also called the Sailors' Church, for the mariners who left behind votive lamps in thanksgiving for safe passage. The attached Musée Marguerite-Bourgeoys tells the story of one of Montréal's early benefactors. The crypt has artifacts dating back 2000 years.

◎ GALERIE LE CHARIOT

☎ 514-875-4994; 446 pl Jacques-Cartier; Ⓜ Champ-de-Mars

This arts emporium claims to have the largest Inuit collection in Canada. Choose from First Nations art carved mainly from soapstone, as well as walrus tusks, fur hats, mountain-goat rugs and fleecy moccasins.

◎ GALERIE ST-DIZIER

☎ 514-845-8411; 24 rue St-Paul Ouest; Ⓜ Champ-de-Mars

This spacious Old Town gallery has always been at the forefront of the contemporary avant-garde scene in Montréal. Works are split between local and heavyweight artists known abroad.

◎ HÔTEL DE VILLE

☎ 514-872-3355; 275 rue Notre-Dame Est; ◷ 8am-5pm Mon-Fri, free tours 10am-4pm late Jun–mid-Aug; Ⓜ Champ-de-Mars

Montréal's striking City Hall, completed in 1878, is steeped in local lore. Most famously, French leader Charles de Gaulle took to the balcony in 1967 and yelled out to the crowds outside *'Vive le Québec libre!'* ('Long live a free Québec!').

Live music at Place Jacques-Cartier

MARCHÉ BONSECOURS
☎ 514-872-7730; 350 rue St-Paul Est;
🕙 10am-6pm Jan-Mar, 10am-6pm
Sat-Wed & 10am-9pm Thu & Fri Apr-Jun
& Labor Day-Dec, 10am-9pm Mon-Sat &
10am-6pm Sun Jul-Labor Day; Ⓜ Champ-
de-Mars
Opened in 1847, this neoclassical
building has been everything
from a farmers market to a concert
theater to a brief stint as city
hall (1852–1878). The marché
reopened in 1992 as a gallery
for shops selling arts and crafts.
Restaurants line the facade on rue
St-Paul.

MUSÉE D'ARCHÉOLOGIE
POINTE-À-CALLIÈRE
☎ 514-872-9150; www.pacmuseum
.qc.ca; 350 Place Royale; admission $14;
🕙 10am-6pm Mon-Fri & 11am-6pm
Sat & Sun late Jun-early Sep, 10am-5pm
Tue-Fri & 11am-5pm Sat & Sun rest of the
year; Ⓜ Place-d'Armes
This excellent museum contains
artifacts and archaeological
ruins dating back to Montréal's
founding in the 17th century.
Before delving into subterranean
galleries, visitors should start
with *Montréal, Tales of a City*, a 20-
minute multimedia show giving a
historical overview of the city. See
p13 for more information.

PLACE JACQUES-CARTIER
The liveliest spot in Old Montréal,
this gently inclined square hums
with performance artists, street
musicians and the animated chat-
ter from terrace restaurants lining
its borders.

OLD PORT
The Old Port is a requisite stop during a visit to Old Montréal. Numerous
sites sit along its four piers, with tourist
cruises embarking from here. In warm
weather the Promenade du Vieux-Port
is a favorite recreation spot for joggers,
in-line skaters and cyclists. In cold
weather you can skate at the outdoor
rink against the backdrop of the St-
Lawrence River.

OLD MONTRÉAL

SAILORS' MEMORIAL CLOCK TOWER

Quai de l'Horloge pier; ⏱ **10am-7pm**
At the east edge of the historic port stands the Tour de l'Horloge. This notable clock commemorates all of the sailors and shipmen who died in the world wars. Visitors can climb the 192 steps for a view over Old Montréal and the river.

YVES LAROCHE GALERIE D'ART *Art Gallery*

☎ **514-393-1999; 4 rue St-Paul Est;** Ⓜ **Champ-de-Mars**
High and low culture collide at this fantastic gallery that showcases the best in upscale contemporary and urban art. With everything from surrealist to pop art, tattoo to illustration, this local institution presents massive collective shows that are held twice a year.

🏃 DO

AML CRUISES *River Cruise*

☎ **1-866-856-6668; www.croisiere saml.com; Quai King-Edward; 1½hr tour $27;** ⏱ **11:30am, 2pm & 4pm;** Ⓜ **Champ-de-Mars**
One of several river cruises offered from the Old Port, AML offers 1½-hour tours in a glassed-in sightseeing boat taking in the Old Port, Île Ste-Hélène and Îles de Boucherville. Other options include evening dining cruises and weekend brunch cruises.

🚴 ÇA ROULE *Cycling*

☎ **514-866-0633; www.caroulemon tréal.com; 27 rue de la Commune est; bikes per hr/day $8/25;** ⏱ **9am-8pm;** Ⓜ **Place-d'Armes**
Near the waterfront, this outfit rents out bikes, tandems, rollerblades and accessories. It's just a few steps away from the bike path

WHEN IN MONTRÉAL...

Montrealers are generally a pretty relaxed bunch, but you'll undoubtedly make a better impression if you observe a few simple rules.

> Always start off in French. It's polite to begin your queries in shops, restaurants and public places with *'Est-ce que vous parlez anglais?'* ('Do you speak English?'), rather than launching straight into English. You might be addressed with *'Bonjourhello'* to suss out your own language preference.

> When walking into a shop, say *'Bonjour'* when you arrive and *'Merci, bonjour'* when you leave.

> Don't address waiters as *'garçon'*, which means 'boy' and is considered rude. Say *'Excusez madame/mademoiselle/monsieur.'*

that follows along the Canal de Lachine for 14km.

☒ CALÈCHE *Carriage Rides*
Place d'Armes; per half-hr/hr $45/75;
Ⓜ **Place-d'Armes**

Sure it's touristy, but if the mood strikes, hop in a carriage and take a ride through the cobblestoned streets of Old Montréal. Drivers can give you an earful of history, and can be found all year long. You can also hire carriages by the waterfront near Place Jacques-Cartier.

☒ PARC DU BASSIN-BONSECOURS
Boating & Ice-skating

☎ **514-282-0586; www.quaisduvieux port.com; Old Port;** ☼ **10am-10pm Jun-Aug, 11am-8pm Sat & Sun May & Sep;** Ⓜ **Champ-de-Mars**

Just east of Quai Jacques Cartier lies this grassy expanse enclosed by a waterway and crisscrossed with footbridges. In summer, you can rent tiny paddleboats ($6.50 per half-hour) or remote-control model sailboats; in winter the ice skaters take over.

Ice-skating at Parc du Bassin-Bonsecours

Take a calèche ride through the streets of Old Montréal

SAUTE MOUTONS *Jet-boating*

☎ 514-284-9607; www.jetboating
montréal.com; Old Port; jet boat $65;
⏱ 10am-6pm May-Oct; M Champ-de-
Mars

Thrill-seekers will get their money's worth on these fast, wet and bouncy boat tours to the Lachine Rapids. The aluminum jet boats take you through foaming white waters, from Quai de l'Horloge, on hour-long tours.

🛍 SHOP

DIFFUSION GRIFF *Fashion*

☎ 514-398-0761; Marché Bonsecours, 350 rue St-Paul Est; M Champ-de-Mars

French fashion diva Anne de Shalla studied fashion in Paris and came to Montréal in the 1970s. She now selects pieces from up to 30 Québec designers every year for the exclusive collection that is showcased in her shop.

LIBRISSIME *Books*

☎ 514-841-0123; 62 rue St-Paul Ouest
M Place-d'Armes

Librissime imports gorgeous books from across the globe. White gloves are laid on the displays for you to don before handling the tomes, including massive books that cost upwards of $1000.

Dimitri Antonopoulos
President of the Société de développement commercial Vieux-Montréal and one of the leaders in the movement to revitalize Old Montréal

Where do you live? In Old Montréal. I walk to work. That's one of the great things about Montréal, you don't need a car. You can walk everywhere. **How has Old Montréal changed since you were a kid?** The streets used to be empty; no one lived down here. Slowly, it started becoming a destination – first for tourists in the summer, but now it's becoming a year-round destination. And some 5000 to 6000 people live in the neighborhood. **What are your hopes for the future of Old Montréal?** I'd like to see more people moving here to live and work, and to see more neighborhood life. The Old Port (p58) will play a role: this is federally controlled land looking to modernize, and it will be an integral part of the city. **Where are you favorite places to go out in the city?** In Old Montréal my favorite spots are here at Suite 701 (p67), L'Orignal (p64) and Garde-Manger (opposite). I also like going out around av du Parc and av du Mont-Royal (Map pp80–1, A2) heading east – lots of cool bars and cafes, and some excellent brunch places.

🏠 REBORN *Fashion*

☎ 514-499-8549; 231 rue St-Paul Ouest; Ⓜ Place-d'Armes

Upscale lines like Harakiri, Complexgeometries, Flippa K, Opening Ceremony and Nom de Guerre meet accessories and a slick, old-meets-new feel at this must-see fashion laboratory.

🍴 EAT

🍴 BORIS BISTRO
Bistro $$

☎ 514-848-9575; 465 rue McGill; mains $16-23; Ⓜ Square-Victoria

This popular place gets packed at lunchtime. Dishes range from artfully presented salads to fantastic duck risotto with mushrooms, along with pasta with spicy chorizo and mahi mahi. Eat in the nicely appointed dining side or in the outdoor courtyard.

🍴 CLUNY ARTBAR *Cafe* $

☎ 514-866-1213; 257 rue Prince; mains $6-9; ⏱ 8:30am-5pm Mon-Wed & Fri, to 7pm Thu; Ⓜ Square-Victoria

Tucked into the loft-like Darling Foundry gallery is this charmingly hip cafe that serves breakfast, lunch (soups, sandwiches, antipasto) and coffee to an artsy-chic, bilingual Old Montréal clientele. It's open later Thursdays for dinner and drinks.

🍴 DA EMMA *Italian* $$

☎ 514-392-1568; 777 rue de la Commune Ouest; mains $15-28; Ⓜ Square-Victoria

The old stone walls and beamed ceiling of this atmospheric place – a former women's prison – today provide the backdrop to delicious Italian cooking. Osso buco, fresh grilled fish, agnolotti with stuffed veal and satisfying homemade pastas are top picks from the changing menu.

🍴 GARDE-MANGER
International $$$

☎ 514-678-5044; 409 rue St-Francois-Xavier; mains $25-35; ⏱ 6pm-3am Tue-Sun; Ⓜ Place-d'Armes

The buzz surrounding Garde-Manger hasn't let up since its opening in 2006. This tiny upscale restaurant attracts a mix of local scenesters who come for the lobster risotto, short ribs, succulent snow crab and other changing specials. After midnight, the restaurant becomes a party place.

🍴 GIBBY'S *Steakhouse* $$$

☎ 514-282-1837; 298 Place d'Youville; mains $30-45; Ⓜ Square-Victoria

A touch on the touristy side, Gibby's nonetheless serves excellent grilled meats and seafood, including a respected rack of lamb. The old-school restaurant is set in a charming stone building dating back to the 1700s.

NEIGHBORHOODS

OLD MONTRÉAL

Slurping soup in Chinatown

🍴 LA GARGOTE *French* $$
☎ 514-844-1428; 351 Place d'Youville; mains $18-26; ⏲ noon-2:30pm & 5:30-10pm; Ⓜ Square-Victoria

An Old Montréal standard, this handsome little place serves quality bistro fare in a dining room with stone walls and beamed ceilings. The lunchtime *table d'hôte* is good value.

🍴 LE CLUB CHASSE ET PECHE *French* $$$
☎ 514-861-1112; 423 rue St-Claude; mains $29-31; Ⓜ Champ-de-Mars

One of the pillars of Old Montréal's grand dining scene, this elegant restaurant serves fantastic

new-wave French fare, including grilled Wagyu beef, sautéed scallops with fennel and a succulent lamb. In the summer at lunchtime, dine al fresco in the historical Château Ramezay garden across the street.

🍴 L'ORIGNAL *French* $$$
☎ 514-303-0479; 479 rue St-Alexis; mains $25-35; ⏲ 6-11pm Mon-Sat; Ⓜ Place-d'Armes

This cozy chalet-style restaurant specializes in exquisitely prepared game meat and fresh seafood. Start off with oysters before moving on to braised wild boar or poached turbot in a lobster bisque. On weekend nights, the place gets packed and attracts a festive crowd when the kitchen closes.

🍴 MARCHÉ DE LA VILLETTE
Deli $

☎ 514-807-8084; 324 rue St-Paul Ouest; sandwiches $7-13, mains $10-20; ☽ 9am-6pm Mon-Fri, to 5pm Sat & Sun; Ⓜ Square-Victoria

Here you'll find a convivial traditional charcuterie serving made-to-order sandwiches with homemade pâté, cured ham, sausages, foie gras and an array of pungent cheeses.

🍴 OLIVE + GOURMANDO
Deli, Bakery $

☎ 514-350-1083; 351 rue St-Paul Ouest; sandwiches from $8-10; ☽ 8am-6pm Tue-Sat; Ⓜ Square-Victoria

This cafe is legendary in town for its sandwiches and baked goods

CHINATOWN

Despite its diminutive size, Montréal's Chinatown percolates with energy. Here you'll find bustling eateries attracting diners from all parts of the globe, incense-filled shops, curio stalls and Taiwanese bubble-tea parlors. Entry to the district is through one of two gold-leaf ceremonial gates, one on blvd St-Laurent and the other at av Viger, both gifts from the city of Shanghai. The main attraction here is the plethora of atmospheric restaurants serving Cantonese, Szechuan and Vietnamese delicacies. St-Laurent and pedestrian-only rue de la Gauchetière (C1) are good starting points in the culinary journey.

One of Montréal's best places for dim sum is **La Maison Kam Fung** (☎ 514-878-2888; 1111 rue St-Urbain; mains $4-13; ☽ 7am-3pm & 5-10pm; Ⓜ Place-d'Armes), especially popular for Saturday and Sunday brunch. The entrance is hidden in the rear of a shopping passage up an escalator.

A favorite local spot is friendly **Beijing** (☎ 514-861-2003; 92 rue de la Gauchetière; mains $8-15; ☽ 11am-3am; Ⓜ Place-d'Armes), which serves an assortment of traditional Cantonese and Szechuan dishes and stays open late. For dessert, step across the street to **Harmonie** (☎ 514-875-1328; 85 rue de la Gauchetière), a Hong Kong–style bakery with custard tarts.

For all-you-can-eat action, head to **Jardin de Jade** (☎ 514-866-3127; 67 rue de la Gauchetière Ouest; buffet $10-14; ☽ 11am-10:30pm daily; Ⓜ Place-d'Armes), a chaotic buffet with vegetarian plates, sushi, dumplings, fish, ribs and more.

Tasty bowls of noodle soup are unmatched at **Phó Bang New York** (☎ 514-954-2032; 970 blvd St-Laurent; mains $9-14; ☽ 10am-10pm; Ⓜ Place-d'Armes). Just up the road, **Hoang Oanh** (☎ 514-954-0053; 1071 blvd St-Laurent; sandwiches $2.75; ☽ 11am-3am; Ⓜ Place-d'Armes) is a great little hole in the wall for fresh Vietnamese *bahn mi* (baguette sandwiches).

Cirque du Soleil sets up its big top in Montréal's Old Port

and gets packed at lunchtime. Fresh-baked loaves feature nicely in the gourmet sandwiches (like trout with herbed cream cheese, capers, spinach and sun-dried tomatoes).

TOQUÉ! *French* $$$
☎ 514-499-2084; 900 place Jean-Paul-Riopelle; mains $40-45; ⏲ 5:30-10:30pm Tue-Sat; Ⓜ Place-d'Armes
Celebrated Chef Normand Laprise has garnered much attention for his fresh, innovative menus that are based on ingredients sourced from local farms. Seven-course tasting menus showcase the variety of rich flavors he brings together.

🍸 DRINK
🍸 CAFÉ DES ÉCLUSIERS
Lounge
☎ 514-496-0109; 400 rue de la Commune Ouest; ⏲ 11:30am-11pm Mon-Wed, Fri & Sat, to 1am Thu; Ⓜ Place-d'Armes
This Old Port summertime staple opens from May to September. Always crowded, it has a restaurant, bar, lounge and sprawling outdoor terrace. Expect a somewhat sceney, after-work crowd, house music and elaborate cocktails.

🍸 PUB ST-PAUL *Pub*
☎ 514-874-0485; 124 rue St-Paul Est; ⏲ 11am-3am; Ⓜ Champs-de-Mars

In the heart of Old Montréal's most touristy drag is this rock pub: a hit among students, jocks and passersby. You'll find upscale pub fare, live bands on weekend nights and nightly drink specials.

Y SUITE 701 *Bar*
☎ 514-904-1201; 701 Côte de la Place d'Armes; ⏰ 5pm-3am; Ⓜ Place-d'Armes

Housed in the former lobby of posh Hotel Place d'Armes, which in turn is located in a former bank, this elegant marble-filled space attracts a well-dressed, somewhat corporate crowd ready for the night to unfold.

Y WUNDERBAR *Lounge*
☎ 514-395-3195; 901 Square Victoria; ⏰ 10pm-3am Wed-Sat; Ⓜ Square-Victoria

Wunderbar was developed by New York–based nightlife impresarios, who blended local and international culture with the ease of a dry martini. Weekly DJ nights attract a dance-loving, trendy crowd.

★ PLAY

★ CHERRY *Club*
☎ 514-841-9669; 417 rue St-Pierre; ⏰ 10pm-3am Thu-Sat; Ⓜ Square-Victoria

Old-school house music and decadent antics are de rigueur at this party spot known for its red-leather booths and on-fire dance floor.

★ CIRQUE DU SOLEIL *Theater*
☎ 514-800-450-1480; www.cirquedusoleil.com

While Cirque's touring shows remain the company's bread and

RAGS TO RICHES: CIRQUE DU SOLEIL

The real-life story of Guy Laliberté is one of the great success stories of Canada. Born in Québec City in 1959, he spent his youth honing his skills at stilt walking, fire breathing and accordion playing. He and a group of like-minded friends struggled to make ends meet as performance artists, until a big break in 1984 when Cirque du Soleil (Circus of the Sun; above) was born.

Success since then has snowballed, with critically acclaimed performances appearing on stages across the globe. Ever true to the simple dictum of using neither animals, nor speech onstage, Laliberté continues to push boundaries in his shows, which blend dance, acrobatics and theater. The megaproduction *O* took place in a 25-foot deep, 1.5million-gallon pool. An underwater crew stayed submerged for the entire 90-minute performance to catch divers and give them hits of oxygen.

Laliberté, the performer who once busked for change is now a billionaire entertainment mogul. He's also a major source of pride for Montrealers — and aspiring artists across the globe.

Tom Lansky, Calèche Driver

Tom, a native Hungarian, and his horse, Silver, have been offering carriage tours around Montréal for over 15 years.

What do you like most about Montréal? The diversity, the people. It's a very cosmopolitan city. The French influence adds a lot. **Are you out here in the winter?** Silver and I are out here all year. There are only about three or four of us (drivers) dumb enough to come out in the winter. Actually we do sleigh rides in the winter up through the Parc du Mont-Royal (p79). **How do you survive the winter?** Just barely. I suffer. I shiver a lot. **Do you take the horse home at night?** No, I ride my bike into work along the Canal de Lachine, which is near the stables. **Any tips for enjoying the city?** See a show – especially Cirque du Soleil (p67), which started here some 25 years ago. Go to the festivals. The Jazz Fest (p26) is great and so is the Comedy Fest (p27). My favorite, though, is the international beer festival (p25), with over 300 different kinds of beer.

butter, Montrealers often enjoy first looks at new shows in the Old Port. Look for the Grand Chapiteau (Big Top) on the Quai Jacques Cartier in the summer. See the boxed text, p67, for more.

⭐ **TRIBE HYPERCLUB** *Club*
☎ 514-845-3066; 390 rue St-Jacques Ouest; 🕙 10pm-3am Thu-Sun; Ⓜ Place-d'Armes

Celebrity guests, such as P-Diddy and Paris Hilton; house, trance and techno DJs; and sexy patrons make this very-hyper nightclub the go-to spot for thousands of people. Don't forget the monstrous 100,000-watt sound system.

>QUARTIER LATIN & THE VILLAGE

The young, boisterous neighborhood of the Quartier Latin is a lively if unpolished district packed with buzzing bars, bistros and record shops. The anchor of the neighborhood is the Université du Québec à Montréal (p72), which brings thousands of students streaming in every day, and gives the neighborhood its vibrancy.

In the 19th century, the neighborhood was an exclusive residential area for wealthy francophones. Although many original buildings burned in the great fire of 1852, there are a number of Victorian and art nouveau gems hidden on the tree-lined streets. Today, the quarter is a hotbed of activity, especially during summer festivals, when energy spills from the streets 24 hours a day.

Gay-friendly doesn't even begin to describe the Village, one of the world's most exuberant communities for people of all persuasions. Packed with eclectic eateries, shops and nightspots, rue Ste-Catherine is the main thoroughfare, and it closes to traffic in the summer. August is the most frenetic time as hundreds of thousands of international visitors gather to celebrate Divers/Cité (p27), the massive annual Gay Pride parade.

QUARTIER LATIN & THE VILLAGE

◉ SEE

◉ ÉCOMUSÉE DU FIER MONDE

☎ 514-528-8444; 2050 rue Amherst; admission $6; ⏱ 11am-8pm Wed, 9:30am-4pm Thu & Fri, 10:30am-5pm Sat & Sun; Ⓜ Berri-UQAM

This magnificent ex-bathhouse explores the history of Centre-Sud, an industrial district of Montréal until the 1950s and now part of the Village. The museum's permanent exhibition puts faces on the Industrial Revolution through excellent displays. Frequent modern-art exhibitions are also held here.

◉ UNIVERSITÉ DU QUÉBEC À MONTRÉAL

☎ 514-596-3000; 405 rue Ste-Catherine Est; Ⓜ Berri-UQAM

The uninspiring buildings of this French-language university aren't winning any design awards, though the old Gothic steeple of the Église St-Jacques has been integrated into the university's facade.

▢ SHOP

▢ ARCHAMBAULT
Books, Music

☎ 514-849-6202; 500 rue Ste-Catherine Est; Ⓜ Berri-UQAM

One of Montréal's oldest and largest book and record shops makes for some fine browsing – and some recordings sold here are nearly impossible to find outside Québec.

▢ LE CHÂTEAU Fashion

☎ 514-279-6391; 6729 rue St-Hubert; Ⓜ Berri-UQAM

TOP ALBUMS FROM QUÉBEC

> Jean Leloup *Le Dôme* (1996) Features the great songwriting of Québec superstar Leloup (sometimes touted as the Lou Reed of Québec), at his mind-blowing best.
> Arcade Fire, *Funeral* (2004) The ground-breaking debut album of this indie-rock band is still considered its best.
> Les Colocs *Les Colocs* (1993) The first album of this much-revered band is full of its unique touches: social criticism, manic energy and a wicked sense of fun.
> DobaCaracol *Soley* (2004) Beautifully textured album by this female duo (who have since split up) that blends African, tribal and folk sounds in its highly enjoyable collection.
> Daniel Bélanger *Quatre Saisons dans le Désordre* (1996) Bélanger creates a complex world that blends jazz and folk with touches of the avant-garde.
> Pierre Lapointe *La Forêt des Mal-Aimés* (2006) Lapointe creates gorgeous music, and is head of a new crop of young talent emerging from Québec.

QUARTIER DE SPECTACLES

One of Montréal's most ambitious urban-renewal projects in recent years is well underway on the edge of the Quartier Latin and eastern Downtown. The project aims to bring new life to this culturally rich area (bordered roughly by rue Berri, rue Sherbrooke, blvd René-Lévesque and City Councillor's street). Currently the 1-sq-km district houses 30 performance halls, numerous galleries and exhibition spaces; it also hosts various big-ticket festivals. The government has pledged $120 million to making the area a more attractive place to live, work and create in hopes of transforming the Quartier into an international destination.

This trendy concept store stocks cheap designer knockoffs, including trendy club wear. There are also a number of other branches around town.

🏠 PRIAPE *Sex, Fetish*
☎ 514-521-8451; 1311 rue Ste-Catherine Est; Ⓜ Beaudry
Montréal's biggest gay sex store has made a career out of parodying itself in great style. You'll find plenty of mainstream erotic wares (DVDs, mags and books), along with shrink-wrap jeans, black leather gear and other titillating accoutrements.

🏠 RENAUD BRAY
Books, Music
☎ 514-876-9119; 1376 rue Ste-Catherine Est; 🕑 9am-midnight; Ⓜ Beaudry
One of 14 branches in greater Montréal, this bright and cheery bookstore specializes in French titles but has a decent choice of English best-sellers, travel and literature titles.

🏠 UNDERWORLD
Fashion, Music
☎ 514-284-6473; 289 rue Ste-Catherine Est; 🕑 10am-6pm Mon-Wed, 10am-10pm Thu & Fri, 11am-5pm Sun
Underworld is a first-class punk refuge and supply house on an appropriately grungy stretch of rue Ste-Catherine. They've got jeans, a big CD and record store in the basement and a great selection of skates and snowboards.

🍴 EAT
🍴 AU PETIT EXTRA
French $$
☎ 514-527-5552; 1690 rue Ontario Est; mains $15-21; 🕑 11:30am-2:30pm & 6-10pm Mon-Wed, 6-10:30pm Thu-Sat, 5:30-9:30pm Sun; Ⓜ Papineau
This sweet little place serves traditional bistro fare to a garrulous local crowd. The blackboard menu

NEIGHBORHOODS

QUARTIER LATIN & THE VILLAGE

Vibrant characters watch over the facade of Kilo cafe

changes frequently but features simple, flavorful dishes (*steak frites*, foie gras, *confit de canard*, mahi mahi), and staff can expertly pair wines with food.

🍴 KILO *Cafe* $
☎ 514-596-3933; 1495 rue Ste-Catherine Est; mains $5-11; ⏲ 5-11pm Mon, 10:30am-11pm Tue-Thu, 10:30am-2am Fri, 1pm-2am Sat, 1-11pm Sun; Ⓜ Papineau

The house specialties are creamy cakes and tarts with a shot of Grand Marnier or some other liquid decadence, as well as hot sandwiches, snacks and salads. It's a great anytime coffee-and-dessert spot.

🍴 LA PARYSE *Diner* $
☎ 514-842-2040; 302 rue Ontario Est; mains $8-10; ⏲ 11am-11pm Mon-Fri, 2-10:30pm Sat & Sun; Ⓜ Berri-UQAM

Often credited with the thickest, juiciest burgers and best fries in town, this smart little retro diner offers a wide variety of toppings and creamy, rich milkshakes.

🍴 LE COMMENSAL *Vegetarian* $
☎ 514-845-2627; 1720 rue St-Denis; buffet per person $10-16; ⏲ 11am-10:30pm; Ⓜ Berri-UQAM

A requisite stop for vegetarian diners in Montréal, this handsomely rustic dining room stocks an impressive variety of high-quality vegetarian cuisine, including baked dishes (lasagna, casseroles, quesadillas), salads and desserts, sold by weight.

🍴 LE SPIRITE LOUNGE
Vegetarian $

☎ 514-522-5353; 1205 rue Ontario Est; meals $16; ⏰ 6pm-midnight Tue-Sun; Ⓜ Beaudry

This eccentric restaurant with over-the-top decor (Christmas lights and tinfoil) is good fun but requires a bit of preparation. There's no menu but the meal consists of soup, a hot crepe and cake. Eat every bite; if you don't, the chef will angrily tell you 'no cake for you!', then deliver the bill and ask you to leave (no kidding!).

🍴 MOZZA *Italian* $$

☎ 514-522-4116; 1208 rue Ste-Catherine Est; mains $16-22; ⏰ 5-10pm Tue-Sun; Ⓜ Beaudry

One of the Village's best-kept secrets, this cozy, tucked-away restaurant serves delicious Caesar salads, thin-crust pizzas and pastas (try the penne à la vodka). Reservations are recommended at this bring-your-own-wine spot.

🍴 O'THYM *French* $$

☎ 514-525-3443; 1112 blvd de Maisonneuve Est; mains $24-31; ⏰ noon-2:30pm Tue-Fri, 6-10pm daily; Ⓜ Beaudry

O'Thym is a delightful new addition to the neighborhood, with an elegant but understated dining room (exposed brick walls, floodlit windows, oversized mirrors), and beautifully presented plates of fresh seafood and grilled game. Bring your own wine.

🍸 DRINK

🍸 CLUB DATE PIANO-BAR
Pub

☎ 514-521-1242; 1218 rue Ste-Catherine Est; ⏰ 8am-3am; Ⓜ Beaudry

This gay tavern knew what they were doing when they Karaoke-fied the spot. A mixed crowd cheers on aspiring vocalists from all walks of life, from hilariously awful to downright star-worthy.

🍸 LE ST-SULPICE *Bar*

☎ 514-844-9458; 1680 rue St-Denis; ⏰ 11am-3am; Ⓜ Berri-UQAM

This student evergreen is spread over four levels in an old Victorian stone house – a cafe, several terraces, disco and a sprawling back garden for warm summer nights.

🍸 LES TROIS BRASSEURS
Pub

☎ 514-845-1660; 1660 rue St-Denis; ⏰ 11am-1am; Ⓜ Berri-UQAM

This chain of European beer brewers has set up a great locale in the Quartier Latin. Four homegrown brews are always on tap and the menu has a number of great bistro-style bites.

☂ QUARTIER LATIN *Pub*
☎ 514-845-3301; 318 rue Ontario Est; ⏱ 3pm-3am; Ⓜ Berri-UQAM

This cool bar with 1950s lounge-style decor has a small dance floor and a DJ playing New Wave on weekends. A great, reliable hangout any night of the week.

☂ SALOON *Bar*
☎ 514-522-1333; 1333 rue Ste-Catherine Est; ⏱ 11:30am-11pm Mon-Fri, 10am-3am Sat & Sun; Ⓜ Beaudry

This recently revamped gay bar-bistro earned a spot in Village hearts for its chilled atmosphere, cocktails and 'five-continents' menu including some good vegetarian options.

☂ STUD BAR *Bar*
☎ 514-598-8243; rue Ste-Catherine Est; ⏱ 10am-3am; Ⓜ Papineau

This Village meat market has poor visibility and lots of guys with no hair and persistent hopes for the night ahead.

★ PLAY
★ BISTRO À JOJO *Live Music*
☎ 514-843-5015; 1627 rue St-Denis; ⏱ 11am-3pm; Ⓜ Berri-UQAM

This smoky venue in the Quartier Latin is the place for down 'n' dirty

French and English blues and rock groups nightly.

★ BOURBON COMPLEX *Club*
☎ 514-268-4679; 1574 rue Ste-Catherine Est; ⏱ 3pm-3am; Ⓜ Beaudry

This gay entertainment complex is big enough to get lost in. There's La Track, a popular disco-bar with a leather boutique, and the Mississippi Club for dancing, live cabaret and drag shows.

★ LE DRUGSTORE *Club*
☎ 514-524-1960; 1366 rue Ste-Catherine Est; ⏱ 8am-3am; Ⓜ Beaudry

This cavernous eight-story space has nine theme bars, boutiques, a large delicatessen and a dance

Le Drugstore has something for everyone

club in the basement. Lesbians and gays stake out their terrain on different floors.

⭐ MADO CABARET *Cabaret*
☎ 514-525-7566; 1115 rue Ste-Catherine Est; ⏱ 2pm-3am; Ⓜ Beaudry

Mado is a local institution, with drag shows featuring an assortment of hilariously sarcastic performers in eye-popping costumes. Shows take place weekends and Tuesday nights.

⭐ PARKING NIGHTCLUB *Club*
☎ 514-282-1199; 1296 rue Amherst; ⏱ 3pm-3am; Ⓜ Berri-UQAM

Located in an old garage repair shop, this multilevel New York–style club is one of the city's best underground dance spots. Though it's definitely a gay cruising joint, it attracts a mixed,

eclectic crowd of dance-ready partiers.

⭐ STEREO *After Hours Club*
☎ 514-286-0325; 858 rue Ste-Catherine Est; ⏱ 2am-11am Fri & Sat; Ⓜ Berri-UQAM

Still featuring an amazing sound system, Stereo attracts everyone – gay, straight, students, drag queens – all looking to lose sleep in style.

⭐ UNITY II *Club*
☎ 514-523-2777; 1171 rue Ste-Catherine Est; ⏱ 10pm-3am Thu-Sun; Ⓜ Beaudry

This old Village favorite tragically burnt down in 2006 but has come back with a bang! The rebuilt version features a club and pub, a kitschy Bamboo bar, pool tables and a rooftop terrace.

>PLATEAU DU MONT ROYAL

East of the verdant Parc du Mont-Royal, the Plateau captures the city's imagination like no other neighborhood. Writers set their novels in it, filmmakers use the photogenic streets as a backdrop, and young Québécois from all over daydream about pulling up stakes and moving here – if only real estate prices weren't so high.

Originally a working-class neighborhood, in the 1960s and '70s the Plateau became the place where writers, singers and all manner of artists lived. The district was made famous by playwright Michel Tremblay who took an unvarnished look at some of its more colorful residents. Pockets of the district were famously poor. But over recent years, gentrification has arrived in full force, transforming the quarter into a highly coveted destination.

The main drags are blvd St-Laurent ('The Main'), rue St-Denis and av du Mont-Royal, with a wealth of sidewalk cafes, restaurants and shops. The

PLATEAU DU MONT ROYAL

◉ SEE
Carré St-Louis 1 D6
Parc du Mont-Royal 2 A3
Parc LaFontaine 3 G4
Théâtre de Verdure 4 F4

◻ SHOP
Coffre aux Trésors du
   Chaînon 5 C3
Duo 6 B6
Kanuk 7 E3
Librairie Michel Fortin .. 8 D6
Preloved 9 B1
Twist Encore 10 B4
U&I 11 B6

⊣⊢ EAT
Au Festin de Babette ... 12 D4
Au Pied de Cochon 13 E4
Aux Vivres 14 C2

Café Santropol 15 B4
Chu Chai 16 D4
Coco Rico .... (see 22)
Jano .... (see 22)
La Sala Rosa 17 B1
L'Express 18 D5
Patati Patata 19 C4
Pintxo 20 D5
Robin des Bois 21 C1
Schwartz's 22 C5

☕ DRINK
Bar Korova 23 B4
Barouf 24 D4
Bily Kun 25 D2
Blizzarts 26 B4
Brûlerie St Denis 27 D4
Chez José 28 D4
GoGo Lounge 29 B6
La Buvette Chez
   Simone 30 A1

Laïka 31 B4
Les Bobards 32 B3
Les Folies 33 E2
Plan B 34 D2
Quai Des Brumes 35 D2
Reservoir 36 C4

★ PLAY
Cactus 37 D2
Café Campus 38 C6
Casa del Popolo 39 C1
Diese Onze 40 D4
La Panthère Noire 41 C6
La Sala Rossa ...... (see 17)
Le Ballatou 42 B3
Le Divan Orange 43 B3
Les Grands Ballets
   Canadiens 44 D1
Tokyo Bar 45 C6

Please see over for map

streets of rue Prince-Arthur and av Duluth are lined with eateries proudly posting placards announcing 'apportez votre vin' (bring your own wine), which only adds to the congenial atmosphere. See p14 for more on this area.

⊙ SEE

⊙ CARRÉ ST-LOUIS

cnr rue St-Denis & rue Prince-Arthur; Ⓜ **Sherbrooke**

This lovely green space with a three-tiered fountain is flanked by beautiful rows of Second Empire homes. In the 19th century a reservoir here was filled, and a neighborhood emerged for well-to-do French families.

⊙ PARC DU MONT-ROYAL

cnr av du Parc & av Cedar; Ⓜ **Mont-Royal**

Southwest of the Plateau, the Parc du Mont-Royal is Montréal's best-loved green space, with trails crisscrossing its 100 hectares and

TAM-TAM JAM

Hippie crowds and tireless percussionists gather every Sunday afternoon in summer for the legendary 'tam-tam' concerts at the edge of Parc du Mont-Royal (above). The action takes place at the Georges-Étienne-Cartier monument opposite Parc Jeanne-Mance, at av du Parc and av Duluth. Vendors are on hand selling sarongs, handmade jewelry and other handicrafts, plus drums and other percussion instruments if you feel like joining in.

leading up and down its wooded slopes. Key points in the park include the picturesque Lac des Castors (Beaver Lake), a 102ft-tall cross, and the magnificent lookout from the Belvédère Chalet. See p15 for more on this park.

⊙ PARC LAFONTAINE

cnr rue Sherbrooke Est & av du Parc LaFontaine; Ⓜ **Sherbrooke**

In the warmer months urbanites flock to this great leafy park to enjoy walking and bicycle paths, the attractive ponds and the general air of relaxation. You can rent paddleboats in the summer and ice-skate in winter. The open-air Théâtre de Verdure draws a relaxed crowd on summer evenings for music, dance and drama performances, plus film screenings.

🛍 SHOP

☐ COFFRE AUX TRÉSORS DU CHAÎNON *Fashion*

☎ **514-843-4354; 4375 blvd St-Laurent;** Ⓜ **St-Laurent, then** 🚌 **55**

One of several fine *friperies* (used clothing stores) in the area, Chaînon has a treasure trove of vintage-hipster apparel. Browse through gold pumps, houndstooth

ties, horn-rimmed glasses and other rare finds.

🏠 DUO *Men's Fashion*
☎ 514-845-0882; 30 rue Prince-Arthur Ouest; Ⓜ Sherbrooke

If you're a suave fellow looking to dress sharp, head directly to this well-stocked little shop. Duo carries hot brands like Swedish suitmaker J Lindeberg, and Canada's own DSquared, as well as designer sneakers and accessories.

🏠 KANUK *Fashion*
☎ 514-527-4494; 485 rue Rachel Est; Ⓜ Mont-Royal

When people in Québec say 'Kanuk' they mean the winter coats that last a lifetime. In addition to jackets designed to keep you warm in -30°C temperatures, Kanuk carries raincoats, backpacks and hiking gear.

🏠 LIBRAIRIE MICHEL FORTIN
Bookstore
☎ 514-849-5719; 3714 rue St-Denis; Ⓜ Sherbrooke

A mecca for lovers of foreign languages, this place has books, audio material and novels in seemingly every language in the world.

🏠 PRELOVED *Fashion*
☎ 514-499-9898; 4832 blvd St-Laurent; Ⓜ Mont-Royal

Recycling takes on a whole new meaning at this adorable old-made-new boutique. Bedsheets are transformed into sundresses, jeans become purses and skirts are reborn as T-shirts.

🏠 TWIST ENCORE *Fashion*
☎ 514-842-1308; 3972 blvd St-Laurent; Ⓜ Sherbrooke

This is another favorite *friperie* because of its small but well-chosen selection. Famous 1940s ties, cowboy and motorcycle boots and eye-catching blouses adorn colorful window displays.

🏠 U&I *Fashion*
☎ 514-844-8788; 3650 blvd St-Laurent; Ⓜ Sherbrooke

Local designers like YSO, Morales and Denis Gagnon are in the spotlight at this award-winning boutique, alongside top labels like Vivienne Westwood and Comme des Garçons.

🍴 EAT

🍽 AU FESTIN DE BABETTE
Ice Cream $
☎ 514-849-0214; 4085 rue St-Denis; ice cream $2-4; ⏲ 10am-6pm Sun-Wed, to 10pm Thu-Sat; Ⓜ Mont-Royal

This charming cafe with sidewalk terrace is famed for its homemade ice cream. The supremely satisfying *crème glacée molle à l'ancienne* is chocolate or vanilla ice cream blended on the spot with fresh fruits and berries (you choose).

🍴 AU PIED DE COCHON
French $$$

☎ 514-281-1114; 536 av Duluth Est; mains $20-45; ⏱ 5pm-midnight Tue-Sun; Ⓜ Sherbrooke

One of Montréal's most-respected restaurants features extravagant pork, duck and steak dishes, along with its signature foie gras dishes. Award-winning chef Martin Picard takes normally heavy dishes and transforms them into works of art. Reservations essential.

🍴 AUX VIVRES *Vegetarian* $

☎ 514-842-3479; 4631 blvd St-Laurent; mains $7-10; ⏱ 11am-11pm Tue-Sun; Ⓜ Mont-Royal

Serving some of Montréal's best vegan fare, Aux Vivres whips up tasty fresh salads, soups and

sandwiches, a hearty daily special and homemade desserts. You can also stop in for fresh juices and teas, and dine alfresco in the back garden.

🍴 CAFÉ SANTROPOL *Cafe* $

☎ 514-842-3110; 3990 rue St-Urbain; mains $6-9; ⏱ 11:30am-midnight; Ⓜ St-Laurent, then 🚌 55

This iconic Montréal eatery is known for its towering and creative sandwiches, its colorful digs, and lush outdoor garden patio. You'll also find excellent salads, soups and coffees.

🍴 CHU CHAI
Vegetarian, Thai $$

☎ 514-843-4194; 4094 rue St-Denis; mains $12-22; Ⓜ Mont-Royal

A stylish but unpretentious restaurant of the mock-meat variety, Chu Chai cooks up an impressive variety of Thai dishes. In the summer,

NECTAR OF THE GODS

Québec produces about three-quarters of the world's maple syrup, which is perhaps why it enjoys such pride of place, appearing on everything from meat and desserts to foie gras, blended with smoothies and of course in maple beer. French settlers began producing it regularly in the 1800s after learning how to make it from maple-tree sap by Canadian Aboriginals. Sap is usually extracted in spring after enzymes convert starch into sugars over the winter. Once the weather warms and the sap starts flowing, Quebecers head to *cabanes à sucre* (sugar shacks) out in the countryside. There they sample the first amber riches of the season and do the taffy pull, where steaming maple syrup is poured into the snow and then scooped up on a popsicle stick once it's cooled.

The French-only website Cabane à Sucre (www.cabaneasucre.org) has information on sugar shacks you can visit, and recipes.

L'Express for sumptious feasts

grab a table on the terrace and choose from plump vegetable-and-mushroom dumplings, crispy seaweed and spiced red curries with vegetarian 'duck', 'chicken' or 'beef'.

🍽 COCO RICO
Roasted Chicken $

☎ 514-849-5554; 3907 blvd St-Laurent; mains $4-8; ⌚ 10am-11pm Mon-Fri, from 9am Sat & Sun; Ⓜ St-Laurent, then 🚌 55

No-frills Coco Rico is a great spot to score fresh barbecued chicken, roasted potatoes and custard tarts. With just a few flimsy bar stools, most people order their bird to go.

🍽 JANO *Portuguese* $$

☎ 514-849-0646; 3883 blvd St-Laurent; mains $14-16; ⌚ 11am-11pm; Ⓜ St-Laurent, then 🚌 55

The scent of charcoal-grilled meats and seafood lingers in the air at this welcoming, family-friendly Portuguese restaurant. The menu features straightforward selections of fresh fish, pork and steak, all grilled to choice tenderness.

🍴 LA SALA ROSA *Spanish* $

☎ 514-844-4227; 4848 blvd St-Laurent; mains $10-16, tapas $5-8; ⏲ 5-11pm Mon-Fri, 10am-3pm & 5-11pm Sat & Sun; Ⓜ St-Laurent, then 🚌 55

This little gem serves five tasty varieties of paella (including vegetarian) as well as numerous tapas dishes and a changing lineup of Spanish specials. On Thursday nights, there's a live flamenco show.

🍴 L'EXPRESS
French Bistro $$

☎ 514-845-5333; 3927 rue St-Denis; mains $14-28; ⏲ 8am-3am; Ⓜ Sherbrooke

With a black-and-white checkered floor, art-deco globe lights and mirrored walls, L'Express seems straight out of Paris. The menu features high-end bistro fare, rich seafood dishes, fresh salads and decadent desserts.

🍴 PATATI PATATA *Québécois* $

☎ 514-844-0216; 4177 blvd St-Laurent; mains $4-7; ⏲ 8am-11pm Mon-Fri, from 11am Sat & Sun; Ⓜ St-Laurent, then 🚌 55

This little hole in the wall is a classic spot in the Plateau. Locals file in (and there's often a line) for *poutine* (fries smothered in cheese curds and gravy), filling sandwiches, borscht and tofu burgers.

🍴 PINTXO *Spanish* $$

☎ 514-844-0222; 256 rue Roy; mains $20-22; ⏲ noon-2pm Wed-Fri & 6-10pm daily; Ⓜ Sherbrooke

Tiny plates of delicious tapas rule the day at this artfully decorated Basque restaurant. Start off your meal by treating your taste buds to the poached octopus carpaccio or scallops with olive tapenade before moving onto heartier plates of duck-breast risotto and lamb shank served with couscous.

🍴 ROBIN DES BOIS
French $$

☎ 514-288-1010; 4653 blvd St-Laurent; mains $16-26; ⏲ noon-10pm Mon-Fri, from 6pm Sat; Ⓜ Mont-Royal

Montréal's own Robin Hood, restaurateur Judy Servay donates all profits and tips from this St-Laurent hotspot to local charities. Ever-changing dishes that are scribbled on the chalkboard could include a succulent venison steak or a creamy wild mushroom risotto.

SMOKED PERFECTION

Called pastrami elsewhere in the world, smoked meat is made by smoking beef brisket with garlic, herbs and spices and then steaming it. The iconic recipe was first introduced to Montréal in the 1900s by Ben Kravitz, a Jewish immigrant from Lithuania, who found success by following the recipe his grandparents used to make beef last longer without refrigeration. There's terrific smoked meat all over the city but Schwartz's (below) is the undisputed king. Reuben Schwartz, a Romanian Jew, opened the soon-to-be Montréal icon in 1928, and it's been going strong ever since. Schwartz's meat goes through a 14-day regime of curing and smoking before landing on your plate after a final three-hour steam.

🍴 SCHWARTZ'S
Smoked Meat $

☎ 514-842-4813; 3895 blvd St-Laurent; mains $5-12; ⏲ 8am-12:30am Sun-Thu, to 1:30am Fri, to 2:30am Sat; Ⓜ St-Laurent, then 🚌 55

This legendary old-time Hebrew deli is widely considered to serve the best smoked meat in Montréal, piled high on sourdough rye bread. You can order it to be served fat, medium (recommended) or lean. Expect long lines. See the boxed text, above, for more information.

🍸 DRINK

🍸 BAR KOROVA *Bar*
☎ 514-904-6444; 3908 blvd St-Laurent; ⏲ 10pm-3am; Ⓜ St-Laurent, then 🚌 55

Boozy, smiley fun with the city's arty Anglo musicians and the girls (and boys) who love them. With DJ nights spinning soul, funk, and rock, impromptu dance parties go down at this no-frills watering hole almost every night.

🍸 BAROUF *Bar*
☎ 514-844-0119; 4171 rue St-Denis; ⏲ 1pm-3am; Ⓜ Mont-Royal

This francophone watering hole is the perfect spot for a drink while cruising the Plateau. There are 25 beers on tap, and, as a bonus, brews can be ordered in giant plastic towers with a tap at the bottom.

🍸 BILY KUN *Bar*
☎ 514-845-5392; 354 av du Mont-Royal Est; ⏲ 3pm-3am; Ⓜ Mont-Royal

One of the pioneers of 'tavern chic,' Bily Kun is a favorite place for locals to hang out for a chilled DJ-spun evening. First-time visitors usually gawk at the ostrich heads that are overlooking the bar.

🍸 BLIZZARTS *Bar*
☎ 514-843-4860; 3956a blvd St-Laurent; ⏲ 8pm-3am; Ⓜ St-Laurent, then 🚌 55

Visit the Plateau's smoked-meat experts, Schwartz's

This bar attracts a friendly crowd that files onto the dance floor from time to time. The local artwork on the walls changes regularly.

Y BRÛLERIE ST-DENIS *Cafe*
☎ 514-286-9158; 3967 rue St-Denis;
🕑 8am-11pm Mon-Fri, 9am-midnight Sat & Sun; Ⓜ Sherbrooke
Grab a seat on the front terrace and enjoy an impressive selection of coffees and drink blends, made from beans roasted fresh daily.

Y CHEZ JOSÉ *Cafe*
☎ 514-845-0693; 173 av Duluth Ouest;
🕑 7am-7pm Mon-Fri, 9am-7pm Sat, 10am-7pm Sun; Ⓜ Sherbrooke

This tiny, colorful cafe serves some of the 'hood's best and strongest espresso (along with breakfasts, seafood soup and Portuguese sausage). A young, bohemian clientele tends to spill onto the sidewalk tables out front.

Y GOGO LOUNGE *Bar*
☎ 514-286-0882; 3682 blvd St-Laurent;
🕑 5pm-3am; Ⓜ St-Laurent, then 🚌 55
The retro-kitsch decor would make Austin Powers proud: '60s psychedelics, flower-power motifs and glistening vinyl. Friendly staff shake martinis and dance on the bar, while DJs get things going in the background.

Y LA BUVETTE CHEZ SIMONE
Restaurant, Bar
☎ 514-750-6577; 4869 av du Parc;
🕐 4pm-3am; Ⓜ Laurier
An artsy-chic crowd of francoph-one *bon vivants* and professionals love this cozy wine bar. The staff know their vino, an extensive list complemented by a gourmet tapas menu. Weekends, the place is jammed from *cinq-á-sept* (5pm to 7pm) and into the wee hours.

Y LAÏKA *Cafe*
☎ 514-842-8088; 4040 blvd St-Laurent;
🕐 9am-3am; Ⓜ St-Laurent, then
🚌 55
This local hotspot is a favorite haunt of the electronic-music and new-media crowds. All laptops and espresso by day, evening brings libations and electronica-spinning DJs.

Y LES BOBARDS *Bar*
☎ 514-987-1174; 4328 blvd St-Laurent;
🕐 3pm-3am; Ⓜ St-Laurent, then 🚌 55
This good-natured bar draws a hyperfun 20s crowd for its sizzling Latin-American beats with French lyrics. It's pretty dead until around 10pm, when it's standing room only.

Y LES FOLIES *Cafe*
☎ 514-528-4343; 70 av du Mont-Royal Est; 🕐 9am-10:30pm Sun-Thu, to 12:30am Fri & Sat; Ⓜ Mont-Royal

A cross between a bar, cafe and club, the self-consciously stylish Folies has a DJ every night spin-ning trendy music and, more importantly, the only sidewalk terrace on av du Mont-Royal.

Y PLAN B *Bar*
☎ 514-845-6060; 327 av du Mont-Royal Est; 🕐 3pm-3am; Ⓜ Mont-Royal
Warm decor, elegant snacks and a trustworthy cocktail menu make this high-end bar a perfect date and/or pick-up spot. A sophisticat-ed French-speaking crowd flocks here after work and on weekends.

Y QUAI DES BRUMES *Bar*
☎ 514-499-0467; 4481 rue St-Denis;
🕐 3pm-3am; Ⓜ Mont-Royal
A Parisian-style cafe with ornate framed mirrors, curlicued moldings and paneling that's been toasted brown by a million cigarettes. This fine venue for live jazz, rock and blues bands also has DJ-spun techno in the upstairs disco.

Y RESERVOIR *Pub*
☎ 514-849-7779; 9 rue Duluth Est;
🕐 3pm-3am Mon, from noon Tue-Fri, from 10:30am Sat & Sun; Ⓜ St-Laurent, then 🚌 55
This low-key, friendly brasserie attracts a mixed crowd that's artsy but unpretentious. The owners brew their own beer, and there's gourmet lunch fare, after-work

snacks and weekend brunch. The 2nd-floor terrace is an added draw in summertime.

⭐ PLAY

⭐ CACTUS *Club*

☎ 514-849-0349; 4461 rue St-Denis; 🕐 10pm-3am Thu-Sat; Ⓜ Mont-Royal

Two floors of infatuation with all things Latin, the Cactus is always packed with dancers ready to strut their stuff. Salsas and merengues are performed with astonishing ease by patrons poured into sexy outfits.

⭐ CAFÉ CAMPUS *Club*

☎ 514-844-1010; 57 rue Prince-Arthur Ouest; 🕐 3pm-3am; Ⓜ Sherbrooke

This eternally popular student club has great live acts, mostly French rock and live québécois bands. In summer, people wander in from the cafes and restaurants along rue Prince-Arthur for music and extra-cheap beer.

⭐ CASA DEL POPOLO
Music, Event Space

☎ 514-284-3804; 4873 blvd St-Laurent; 🕐 noon-3am; Ⓜ St-Laurent, then 🚌 55

One of Montréal's sweetest live venues, this place is also known for its vegetarian platters, talented DJs and eclectic lineup of art shows, spoken-word perform-ances and art-house cinema.

⭐ DIESE ONZE *Jazz*

☎ 514-223-3543; www.dieseonze .com; 4115 rue St-Denis; 🕐 varies; Ⓜ Mont-Royal

An essential address for jazz lovers, this subterranean club assembles a well-curated selection of the city's up-and-coming stars. In addition to the main room, there's an open-air terrace, where some shows are staged on warm evenings.

⭐ LA PANTHÈRE NOIRE *Club*

3519 blvd St-Laurent; Ⓜ St-Laurent, then 🚌 55

This glamorous little club brings new-school party kids who dance and drink the night away to Italo-disco, electro and house by local and international DJs.

⭐ LA SALA ROSSA *Live Music*

☎ 514-284-0122; 4848 blvd St-Laurent; Ⓜ Mont-Royal, then 🚌 55

This lovely old performance hall is known for the touring bands that take the stage. Housed in a former community centre, the venue is affiliated with the Spanish bar and tapas restaurant downstairs (p85).

⭐ LE BALLATOU *Club*

☎ 514-845-5447; 4372 blvd St-Laurent; 🕐 9pm-2am Tue-Sun; Ⓜ Mont-Royal

This Afro-Caribbean nightclub draws a multiethnic crowd and sophisticated dancers. Shows are on weeknights for a varied cover;

Eric Khayat

Québec City–born saxophonist, composer and arranger with a regular gig at the House of Jazz among other spots. His first album, Revolución, came out in 2008.

What attracted you to Montréal? Québec City is a small place. If you want to play, the action is in Montréal. **How would you describe the music scene here?** It's a tough place to make it as a musician but you can always get gigs if you diversify yourself – play all kinds of contexts. **Where are the best spots to hear music?** There are three main places, House of Jazz (p52), Jazz Upstairs (p53) and Diese Onze (p89). **What keeps you here?** The city. The people. The vibe. A beach is a beach, but when you find people you connect with, that's what makes you want to stay. **Who are your musical influences?** I'm somewhat of a cross between Dexter Gordon, Maceo Parker and Lenny Pickett. I'm a fan of Stevie Wonder, Tower of Power, Chopin, Bach – it's beautiful music. As a songwriter, this is what I aim for – if music touches you, affects you on some deeper level, then I know I've succeeded.

on weekends the cover (around $7) includes one drink.

⭐ LE DIVAN ORANGE
Restaurant, Music Space

☎ 514-840-9090; 4234 blvd St-Laurent;
🕑 4pm-3am Tue-Sat; Ⓜ St-Laurent,
then 🚌 55

This space was launched as a kind of restaurant-entertainment venue co-op. The artistic vibe is palpable; on any given night there may be a DJ, world-music performer or record launch.

⭐ LES GRANDS BALLETS CANADIENS *Dance*

☎ 514-849-8681; www.grandsballets
.qc.ca; 4816 rue Rivard

Québec's leading ballet troupe stages four performances annually and showcases the best in classical and modern dance. Programs are both innovative and accessible to general audiences.

⭐ TOKYO BAR *Club*

☎ 514-842-6838; 3709 blvd St-Laurent;
🕑 10pm-3am; Ⓜ Sherbrooke

This little club reels in scenesters and suburbanites in their 20s and early 30s, who dance up a storm on two dance floors. The huge rooftop bar and patio makes a fine retreat on summer nights.

>LITTLE ITALY, MILE END & OUTREMONT

The zest and flavor of the old country find their way into lively Little Italy, where the espresso seems stiffer, the pasta sauce thicker and the chefs plumper. Italian football games seem to be broadcast straight onto blvd St-Laurent (C2), where the green-white-red flag is proudly displayed. Drink in the atmosphere on a stroll and don't miss the magnificent Jean-Talon market, always humming with activity.

Dubbed 'the new Plateau' by the exodus of students and artists seeking a more-affordable, less-polished hangout, the Mile End has become a trendsetter in its own right, with upscale dining along av Laurier (B6), the best bagels in town and increasingly trendy hangouts at its epicenter: rue St-Viateur (B5) and blvd St-Laurent (C5).

LITTLE ITALY, MILE END & OUTREMONT

SEE
Église Madonna della Difesa	1	C2
St Michael's & St Anthony's Church	2	B5

SHOP
Au Papier Japonais	3	C6
Billie	(see 19)	
General 54	4	C5
Jet-Setter	5	C6
Le Marché des Saveurs	6	C2
Local 23	7	C4
Mimi & Coco	8	B6
Un Amour des Thés	9	A4

EAT
Alati-Caserta	10	C2
Fairmount Bagel	11	C6
Il Mulino	12	C2
La Khaïma	13	B6
La Moulerie	14	A4
Le Bilboquet	15	A4
Le Cagibi Café	16	C5
Le Petit Alep	17	C1
Marché Jean Talon	18	C2
PhayaThai	19	B6
Pizzeria Napoletana	20	C2
Senzala	21	B4
St-Viateur Bagel	22	B5

DRINK
Bond Lounge Grill	23	B5
Bu	24	C5
Café Olímpico	25	B5
Caffè Italia	26	C2
Chez Serge	27	C5
Dieu du Ciel	28	C6
La Croissanterie Figaro	29	C5
Le Club Social	30	B5
Whiskey Café	31	C4

PLAY
Baldwin Barmacie	(see 19)	
Green Room	32	C5
Il Motore	33	B1
Zoobizarre	34	D3

Outremont is largely a residence for wealthy francophones, with few attractions aside from pretty streets and some upscale dining and shopping. Fabulous old mansions and oversized family homes lie on leafy streets northwest of rue Bernard (A4). There is also a significant Hasidic community though most of the synagogues and community centers are in neighboring Mile End.

👁 SEE

👁 ÉGLISE MADONNA DELLA DIFESA

6800 av Henri-Julien; Ⓜ Jean-Talon

Our Lady of Protection Church was built in 1919 according to the drawings of Florence-born Guido Nincheri (1885-1973), who spent two decades working on the decor of the Roman-Byzantine structure. The artist painted the church's remarkable frescoes, including one of Mussolini on horseback with his generals in the background. The controversial fresco sits above the high marble altar.

👁 ST MICHAEL'S & ST ANTHONY'S CHURCH

5580 rue St-Urbain; Ⓜ Rosemont

This Byzantine-style church positively dominates its corner of St-Urbain and St-Viateur. Its dome and soaring turret make it one of the more unique examples of church architecture in Montréal. Completed by 1915, it has since mainly served the Irish and Polish Catholic communities.

🛍 SHOP

🛍 AU PAPIER JAPONAIS *Origami*

☎ 514-276-6863; 24 av Fairmount Ouest; Ⓜ Laurier

You'd never have guessed how many guises Japanese paper can come in until you visit this gorgeous little shop. The lamps and kites make great gifts and you can fold them for easy transport.

🛍 BILLIE *Fashion*

☎ 514-270-5415; 141 av Laurier Ouest; Ⓜ Laurier

Carefully selected Brazilian shoes, imported dresses, designer jeans, jewelry and luxurious cashmere sweaters make this treasure-filled boutique a must-see on the fashion circuit. Prices aren't cheap but the fits and high fashion are worth the cost.

🛍 GENERAL 54 *Fashion*

☎ 514-270-9333; 54 rue St-Viateur Ouest; Ⓜ Laurier

Mile End artists have created almost everything stocked at this great little boutique. You'll find stuff you won't find anywhere else including funky T-Shirts, snazzy hats and leather handbags.

◪ JET-SETTER *Travel Goods*
☎ 514-271-5058, 800-271-5058; 66 av Laurier Ouest; Ⓜ Laurier

An orgy of state-of-the-art luggage and every travel gadget known to man, Jet-Setter stocks luggage alarms, pocket-sized T-Shirts, 'dry-in-an-instant' underwear and towels, mini-irons and hairdryers.

◪ LE MARCHÉ DES SAVEURS
Gourmet Food
☎ 514-271-3811; 280 pl du Marché du Nord; ☽ 9am-6pm; Ⓜ Jean-Talon

Everything here is québécois, from the food to the handmade soaps to one of the best collections of artisanal local beer in the city. The store was established so local producers could get wider exposure for their regional products, and it's a joy to browse.

Late grape harvest wines for sale at regional produce specialist Le Marché des Saveurs

🛍 LOCAL 23 *Fashion*
☎ 514-270-9333; 23 rue Bernard Ouest;
Ⓜ Laurier
This tart little *friperie* (used clothing store) stocks recycled clothing and heaps of interesting vintage finds. Even if you are not a secondhand-clothing junkie, the well-curated selection makes for a rewarding visit.

🛍 MIMI & COCO *Fashion*
☎ 514-906-0349; 201 av Laurier Ouest;
Ⓜ Laurier
The third boutique of this elegant T-shirt brand sells the Mimi & Coco line, plus leather goods, dresses, knits and chic sportswear for men, women and children. Mandy's on-site salad bar serves tasty snacks and lunchtime treats.

🛍 UN AMOUR DES THÉS
Tea Shop
☎ 514-279-2999; 1224 av Bernard
Ouest; Ⓜ Rosemont
Over 160 types of tea sit in canisters behind the counter of this charming shop. It stocks old favorites plus unusual varieties (tea with chocolate oils, cream of Earl Grey).

🍴 EAT

🍴 ALATI-CASERTA *Bakery* $
☎ 514-271-3013; 277 rue Dante; dessert $3-5; 🕑 10am-5pm Mon, 8am-8pm Tue-Fri, 8am-6pm Sat & Sun; Ⓜ Jean-Talon
For over four decades, this marvelous family-owned pastry shop in Little Italy has wowed Montrealers with its deliciously decadent cannoli, tiramisu and *sfogliatella* (shell- or cone-shaped filled pastries). Master baker Ernesto Bellinfante prepares many types of pastries and cakes each day; arrive early for the best selection.

🍴 FAIRMOUNT BAGEL
Bagels $
☎ 514-272-0667; 74 av Fairmount Ouest; bagels $0.80; 🕑 24hr; Ⓜ Laurier
One of Montréal's famed bagel places, Fairmount offers 20 varieties of bagels, all hand-rolled and baked in a wood-burning oven. People flood in around the clock to scoop them up hot from the oven.

🍴 IL MULINO *Italian* $$
☎ 514-273-5776; 236 rue St-Zotique Est; mains $18-28; 🕑 6-10pm Tue-Sat; Ⓜ Jean-Talon
One of Montréal's best Italian restaurants, this family-style eatery

PARDON?
Menus in Montréal are increasingly bilingual but if you need help with *le français*, don't be shy to ask (the waiters are used to it). Important note: in French, an *entrée* is an appetizer, not a main course – that's *le plat principal*.

Fairmount Bagel

serves a delectable selection of traditional and inventive dishes, all featuring market-fresh ingredients. Grilled vegetables, homemade gnocchi, roast lamb, fresh grilled fish, and tiramisu make for a fantastic meal.

LA KHAÏMA
Mauritanian $$
☎ 514-948-9993; 142 av Fairmount Ouest; mains $14-18; ⏲ 6pm-midnight; Ⓜ Laurier
For a taste of West Africa, head to this warm and welcoming Maurit-

anian spot. The friendly owner, in traditional dress, cooks up tasty slow-cooked recipes like spiced lentil soup and lamb or vegetables in peanut sauce over couscous. The menu changes regularly and features only a few dishes per day.

LA MOULERIE *Mussels* $$
☎ 514-273-8132; 1249 rue Bernard Ouest; mains $16-22; ⏲ 11:30am-11pm Mon- Fri, from 10am Sat & Sun; Ⓜ Outremont
The mussels here seem bigger than elsewhere and the restaurant

Food-lovers' heaven, Marché Jean-Talon

is renowned for its almost two-dozen sorts. Try the Greek mussels, starring feta and ouzo, or the Indian version with coriander and ginger. There's dining on the front terrace.

🍴 LE BILBOQUET *Ice cream* $
☎ 514-276-0414; 1311 rue Bernard Ouest; cones $3-6; ⏱ noon-midnight; Ⓜ Laurier

A legendary institution in Montréal, Le Bilboquet whips up highly addictive homemade ice-cream and refreshing sorbets. Expect long lines snaking out the door on warm summer nights.

🍴 LE CAGIBI CAFÉ
Vegetarian $
☎ 514-509-1199; 5490 blvd St-Laurent; mains $7-10; ⏱ 10:30am-2:30am; Ⓜ Laurier

Music-loving bohemians and Plateau eccentrics hold court at this plant- and antique-filled vegetarian restaurant by day, bar by night. The menu features tasty soups, salads and Tex-Mex fare.

There's a good entertainment lineup by night (DJs, live bands, film screenings).

⛏ LE PETIT ALEP
Middle Eastern $$

☎ 514-270-9361; 191 rue Jean-Talon Est; mains $10-25; ⏱ bistro 11am-11pm Tue-Sat, restaurant 5-10pm Tue-Sat; Ⓜ De Castelnau

The complex flavors of Syrian-Armenian cuisine draw clientele from all over Montréal. There's hummus, salads, beef kebabs, vegetarian platters and *muhammara* (a walnut, garlic and pomegranate-infused spread). Dine in the bright bistro or the slightly swish dining room next door.

⛏ MARCHÉ JEAN-TALON
Market $

☎ 514-277-1588; 7075 av Casgrain; ⏱ 7am-8pm Mon-Fri, to 6pm Sat & Sun; Ⓜ Jean-Talon

This huge covered market is Montréal's most impressive. Its aisles are packed with merchants selling fruit, vegetables, fresh breads, cheeses and baked goods. The market is flanked by delis and cafe-restaurants with tiny patios.

⛏ PHAYATHAI *Thai* $$

☎ 514-272-3456; 107 av Laurier Ouest; mains $10-18; ⏱ noon-2:30pm & 5.30-10:30pm; Ⓜ Laurier

Although the vote is out on who serves the city's best Thai food, this little restaurant on Laurier is a strong contender. It's hard to go wrong with anything on the menu, with flavorful seafood soup, tender roasted duck and whole red snapper basted in red chili.

⛏ PIZZERIA NAPOLETANA
Italian $

☎ 514-276-8226; 189 rue Dante; mains $9.50-15.50; ⏱ 11am-midnight Mon-Sat, from noon Sun; Ⓜ De Castelnau

RETURN OF THE MONTRÉAL MELON

In its heyday it was truly the Queen of Melons. A single specimen might easily have reached 20lb (9kg), and its spicy flavor earned it the nickname 'Nutmeg Melon.' The market gardeners of western Montréal did a booming business in the fruit.

After WWII small plots vanished as Montréal expanded, and industrial farms had little interest in growing a melon with ultrasensitive rind. By the 1950s the melon was gone – but not forever. In 1996 an enterprising Montréal journalist tracked down Montréal Melon seeds held in a US Department of Agriculture collection in Iowa. The first new crop was harvested a year later in a new collective garden in Notre-Dame-de-Grâce, the heart of the old melon-growing district. To sample this blast from the past, visit local markets such as Marché Atwater (p49) or Marché Jean-Talon (above) after the harvest in September.

St-Viateur Bagel

Homemade pasta sauces and thick-sauced pizzas draw pizza lovers from across the city. The dining room is simple with wooden tables and chairs, and long crowds stretch out the door in the summer.

🍴 SENZALA
Brazilian $$
☎ 514-274-1464; 177 rue Bernard Ouest; mains $12-18; ⏲ 6-10pm Mon-Wed, 9am-late Thu-Sun; Ⓜ Place-des-Arts, then 🚌 80
This colorful restaurant cooks up tasty Brazilian dishes, including flavorful *moqueca* (seafood stew with coconut), and sizzling platters of grilled beef, chicken and shrimp. Weekend brunches are also good.

🍴 ST-VIATEUR BAGEL
Bagels $
☎ 514-276-8044; 263 av St-Viateur Ouest; bagels $0.80; ⏲ 24 hr; Ⓜ Place-des-Arts, then 🚌 80
This place has a reputation stretching across Canada and beyond for its perfectly crusty, chewy and slightly sweet creations, which are served hot from the oven.

▼ DRINK

▼ BOND LOUNGE GRILL
Restaurant, Bar

☎ 514-759-6607; 101 rue Fairmount Ouest; ⏰ 11am-1am Mon-Wed, 11am-3am Thu & Fri, 10am-3am Sat, 10am-1am Sun; Ⓜ Laurier

Plush couches, comfy booths and a long bar make this tapas restaurant a chic-yet-affordable lounge where everyone feels welcome. Ideal for large groups, the kitchen is open late and an outdoor smoking balcony lets you puff away year-round.

▼ BU *Restaurant, Bar*

☎ 514-276-0249; 5245 blvd St-Laurent; ⏰ 5pm-1am; Ⓜ Laurier

This elegant, Italy-inspired wine bar is where Montréal's real wine aficionados go to drink. The 500-strong list features approximately 25 choices by the glass, and the kitchen whips up fine Italian anti-pasti dishes.

▼ CAFÉ OLÍMPICO *Cafe*

☎ 514-495-0746; 124 rue St-Viateur Ouest; ⏰ 7am-11:30pm; Ⓜ Laurier

Its espresso drinks are tops, yet this no-frills Italian cafe is all about atmosphere, with hipsters rubbing elbows with elderly gentlemen and quirky regulars. There's great people-watching from the outdoor terrace.

▼ CAFFÈ ITALIA *Cafe*

☎ 514-495-0059; 6840 blvd St-Laurent; ⏰ 6am-11pm; Ⓜ Jean-Talon

This old-time Italian cafe has a loyal neighborhood following for its unpretentious charm. Plain Formica counters and faded Italian soccer posters set the stage for lingering over excellent espresso and unfussy sandwiches.

QUÉBEC'S TOP ARTISANAL BEERS

> **Boréale** – has everything from black beer to blond, but the red variety is by far the most popular.
> **L'Alchimiste** – this Joliette-based brewer (about 60km northeast of Montréal) turns out a stable of different brews but its Bock de Joliette, an amber beer, is the star of the bunch.
> **Lion D'Or** – this Lennoxville brewer is one of the best in the province and does an outstanding, *very* bitter, bitter beer.
> **McAuslan Brewing** – keep an eye out for its apricot wheat ale and especially its St-Ambroise oatmeal stout
> **Unibroue** – *Fin du Monde* (the End of the World) is a triple-fermented monster with 9% alcohol that more than lives up to its name, and *La Maudite* (the Damned) is a rich spicy beer that clocks in a close second at 8%.

NEIGHBORHOODS

LITTLE ITALY, MILE END & OUTREMONT

☿ CHEZ SERGE Bar
☎ 514-270-3262; 5301 blvd St-Laurent;
☽ 5pm-3am Mon-Sat; Ⓜ St-Laurent,
then 🚌 55

Hockey games, unbridled kitsch and a mechanical bull reel in neighborhood kids, jocks and sports fans who are hankering for the bells and whistles of the sports arena – without actually being there.

☿ DIEU DU CIEL Pub
☎ 514-490-9555; 29 av Laurier Ouest;
☽ 3pm-3am; Ⓜ Laurier

Packed every night with a young, francophone crowd of students, this unpretentious bar serves a phenomenal rotating menu of microbrew beers.

☿ LA CROISSANTERIE FIGARO Cafe
☎ 514-278-6567; 5300 rue Hutchison;
☽ 7am-1am; Ⓜ Laurier

Although this place can get packed, La Croissanterie, with its outdoor terrace, is a lovely spot to nurse a coffee or cocktail. They also serve homemade croissants, salads and other goodies.

☿ LE CLUB SOCIAL Cafe
☎ 514-495-0114; 180 rue St-Viateur Ouest; ☽ 8am-2am; Ⓜ Laurier

Another character-filled cafe, Le Club Social offers a similar formula of success as its rival Olímpico

(p101): a sun-kissed terrace, great coffee and lively ambience.

☿ WHISKEY CAFÉ Lounge
☎ 514-278-2646; 5800 blvd St-Laurent;
☽ 5pm-3am Mon-Fri, from 6pm Sat, from 7pm Sun; Ⓜ St-Laurent, then 🚌 55

Cuban cigars and fine whiskeys are partners in crime at this classy, hidden joint. The well-ventilated cigar lounge is separated from the main bar, which stocks 150 scotch whiskeys, plus wines, ports and tasting trios.

★ PLAY

★ BALDWIN BARMACIE Club
☎ 514-276-4282; 115 av Laurier Ouest;
☽ 5pm-3am Mon-Sat, from 7pm Sun;
Ⓜ Laurier

Loud music, live DJs and beautiful 20- and 30-somethings rule this small, apothecary-themed lounge and club. Showy staff mix specialty cocktails while poppy 1960s-inspired design adds to the fun.

★ GREEN ROOM Bar
☎ 514-284-6665; 5386 blvd St-Laurent;
☽ 9pm-3am; Ⓜ St-Laurent, then 🚌 55

Attitude-free DJs get this small bar hopping on weekends, and a loyal crowd of music-scene partiers, pub crawlers and Anglo hipsters packs the tiny dance floor. Occasional rock and pop shows feature local and out-of-town bands.

⭐ IL MOTORE *Live Music*
☎ 514-284-0122; 179 rue Jean-Talon Ouest; Ⓜ De Castelnau
Hidden in an unsuspecting warehouse building, this well-planned space is perfect for catching the latest indie-rock, alternative and pop acts.

⭐ ZOOBIZARRE *Club*
☎ 514-270-9331; 6388 rue St-Hubert; Ⓜ Rosemont
One of Montréal's coolest party rooms, this venue hosts special DJ nights and concerts featuring local and international talents.

>PARC JEAN-DRAPEAU

In the middle of the mighty St-Lawrence, this alluring green space spreads across Île Ste-Hélène and Île Notre-Dame. Together, the two islands offer an excellent choice of recreational activities, along with some worthwhile museums.

On warm summer days, cyclists, joggers and in-line skaters zoom around the islands. Others opt for a peaceful stroll amid rose gardens and along tiny canals, with splendid views of Montréal and the churning St-Lawrence in the background. In addition to offering a peaceful setting for heading outdoors, the park is home to a Vegas-sized casino, a Formula One racetrack, an old-fashioned amusement park, an artificial beach with lake swimming and a popular electronic-music festival in the summer.

The best way to get around the park is by bicycle – access is via the busy Pont Jacques-Cartier bridge (C2) or via the Cité du Havre (A3). There's also a métro stop on Île Ste-Hélène, plus ferry access in the summer. Information kiosks open during the summer and provide detailed info on upcoming events.

PARC JEAN-DRAPEAU

◉ SEE

◉ BIOSPHÈRE

☎ 514-283-5000; biosphere.ec.gc.ca; Île Ste-Hélène; admission $10; ⏲ 10am-6pm Jun-Oct, 10am-6pm Tue-Sun Nov-May; Ⓜ Jean-Drapeau

Located in the striking spherical dome of the former American pavilion in the '67 World's Fair, this center has the most spectacular collection of hands-on displays in the entire city. Exhibits focus on the world of water, the St-Lawrence River ecosystem and emerging ecotechnologies. Though primarily geared to kids, big people will also find it worthwhile.

◉ HABITAT '67
Cité-du-Havre

The artificial peninsula called Cité-du-Havre was created to protect the port from vicious currents and ice. Here, in 1967, architect Moshe Safdie designed a set of futuristic condominiums (still in use) for the World's Fair, when he was just 23 years old. The narrow spit of land connects Île Ste-Hélène with Old Montréal via the bridge Pont de la Concorde. See the boxed text, below, for more on Safdie.

◉ JARDINS DES FLORALIES
Île Notre-Dame

Take in a bit of a floral beauty wandering the paths of these 25-hectare gardens. Some 5000 rose bushes and 100,000 annuals bloom in the warmer months.

◉ L'HOMME
Île Ste-Hélène

There's a wealth of public art scattered around the islands, including an iconic sculpture created by American artist Alexander

---

THE VISIONARY ARCHITECT FROM MCGILL

Born in Haifa, Israel in 1938, Moshe Safdie graduated from McGill University's architecture program in 1961 and launched quickly to stardom. He was only 23 when asked to design Habitat '67 (above), which was actually based on his university thesis. Since then, Safdie has gravitated towards high-profile, often-controversial projects.

Most notably, Safdie designed the $56-million, 4000-sq-meter Holocaust Memorial in Jerusalem, Israel, that opened in 2005. He also designed Vancouver Library Square, modeled on the dramatic Roman Coliseum, and Ottawa's National Gallery of Canada, with its soaring glass facade. In Montréal, his other famous design was the Jean-Noël Desmarais Pavilion, the evocative modern annex of the Musée des Beaux-Arts (p43).

Although no longer a Montréal resident, Safdie continues to earn praise from his old hometown. He was made a companion of the Order of Canada in 2005, Canada's highest civilian honor.

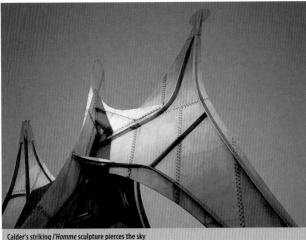

Calder's striking *l'Homme* sculpture pierces the sky

Calder for Expo '67. To those who know the artist's mobiles, the style will be familiar. It is located on the belvedere on the north shore of Île Ste-Hélène, facing the river.

MUSÉE STEWART

☎ 514-861-6701; www.stewart-museum.org; Île Ste-Hélène; admission $11; ☺ 10am-5pm late May-early Oct, 10am-5pm Wed-Mon early Oct-late May; Ⓜ Jean-Drapeau

Inside a former British fort, this museum displays relics from Canada's past as well as a multimedia model of Old Montréal. Demonstrations are given outside

by actors in period costume, and there's a military parade every day in summer.

DO

CIRCUIT GILLES-VILLENEUVE *Racetrack*

Île Notre-Dame

Although Montréal lost the Formula One Grand Prix formerly held on this racetrack (but is trying to get it back), in-line skaters and cyclists can zip around it while taking in the pretty scenery. There's currently no place to rent gear on the islands, so come prepared (try Ça Roule, p59, in Old Montréal).

Strike it rich at Québec's largest casino, Casino de Montréal

🎡 LA RONDE *Amusement Park*

☎ 514-397-2000; www.laronde.com; Île Ste-Hélène; admission $39; 🕙 11am-8pm Jun-Aug; Ⓜ Jean-Drapeau, then 🚌 169; Ⓟ $13

Québec's largest amusement park, La Ronde has a battery of impressive rides including Le Monstre, the world's highest wooden roller coaster and Le Vampire, a corkscrew roller coaster with gut-wrenching turns. Concerts and shows are held throughout the summer, and fireworks explode overhead on weekend evenings.

🎡 PLAGE DES ÎLES *Beach*

☎ 514-872-6093; Île Notre-Dame; admission $8; 🕙 10am-7pm, late Jun-late Aug; 🚌 167

On pretty summer days this artificial sandy beach on the Lac des Regates can accommodate up to 5000 sunning and splashing souls. It's safe, clean and ideal for kids; other attractions include beach volleyball, picnic facilities and snack bars.

🍴 EAT

🍴 NUANCES

International $$$

☎ 514-392-2746; 1 av du Casino, Île Notre-Dame; mains $40-45; 🕙 6-10pm; Ⓜ Jean-Drapeau, then 🚌 167; Ⓟ

Inside the Casino de Montréal, this highly polished, award-winning restaurant, with lovely views of the city skyline, serves delectable fare:

scampi risotto, blackened Alaska cod and Québec lamb wrapped in a savory herb crust are among the standouts. Reservations are essential.

⭐ PLAY
⭐ CASINO DE MONTRÉAL
Casino

☎ 514-392-2746; 1 av du Casino, Île Notre-Dame; ⏰ 24hr; Ⓜ Jean-Drapeau, then 🚌 167

Based in the former French pavilion from the World's Fair, the Montréal Casino (Québec's largest)

opened in 1993 and was an instant success. You can gather your winnings at 3000 slot machines and 120 gaming tables, but drinking isn't allowed on the floor.

⭐ PIKNIC ÉLECTRONIK *DJs*

www.piknicelectronik.com; Belvedere, Île Ste-Hélène; admission $10; ⏰ 1-8pm Sun mid-May–Sep

Dance-lovers flock to this popular outdoor dance party, now in its seventh year. DJs spin a range of eclectronica while you can dance or lounge in the grass.

>QUÉBEC CITY

Québec City is a captivating place whose compact size and historic streets make for some fascinating exploring. The Old Town is packed with museums, old architecture and fantastic scenery.

Parts of the city enjoy a strategic position atop the cliffs of Cap Diamant (Cape Diamond). Quebecers call the upper part the Haute Ville (Upper Town) and the lower part Basse Ville (Lower Town). Together, the 10 sq km of these historic upper and lower areas, within the stone walls, form the Vieux-Québec (Old Town).

The Citadelle, a fort and landmark, stands on the highest point of Cap Diamant. The other major landmark is the splendid, dominating, copper-topped, castle-style Fairmont Le Château Frontenac hotel dating from 1892. Behind the château, a large boardwalk called the Terrasse Dufferin edges along the cliff, providing fabulous views across the river. Below Château Frontenac is Old Lower Town, the oldest section of the city. For more on the city, also see p21.

OLD TOWN

🅒 SEE

🏃 DO

🅢 SHOP

🍴 EAT

🍸 DRINK

⭐ PLAY

SEE

BASILIQUE-CATHÉDRALE NOTRE-DAME-DE-QUÉBEC

Map p111; ☎ 418-694-0665; 20 rue de Buade; admission free, crypt $1; ⏰ 8am-4pm Mon-Fri, to 6pm Sat & Sun; 🚌 3, 7, 11

This basilica, which began life as a humble church in 1647, was gradually enlarged over the years (and repaired following damages during British–French warfare) until reaching its present glory in 1925.

CENTRE D'INTERPRETATION DE PLACE-ROYALE

Map p111; ☎ 418-646-3167; 27 rue Notre-Dame; admission $6; ⏰ 9:30am-5pm late Jun-early Sep, from 10am Tue-Sun early Sep-late Jun; 🚌 1

This sleek interpretive center touts the area as the cradle of French history. The exhibits focus on the individual people, houses and challenges of setting up on the shores of the St-Lawrence River.

ÉGLISE NOTRE-DAME-DES-VICTOIRES

Map p111; ☎ 418-692-1650; 32 rue Sous-le-Fort; admission free; ⏰ 9:30am-4:30pm; 🚌 1

Dating from 1688, this modest house of worship is the oldest stone church in North America. It stands on the spot where de

The majestic interior of Basilique-Cathédrale Notre-Dame-de-Québec

REBIRTH OF ST-ROCH

Once a gritty area better left unexplored, the neighborhood of St-Roch (Map p114) has gone through a remarkable rebirth in the last decade. Under an ambitious revitalization plan, the city created a public garden, restored a shuttered theater and hired artists to paint frescoes in the neighborhood. Artists and entrepreneurs began moving back into the area, bringing cafes and shops on their heels. Today, *le nouveau* St-Roch has become one of Québec City's trendiest neighborhoods. Rue St-Joseph (Map p114, A2) has everything from art galleries and glitzy boutiques to junk shops and fine dining – all drawing a similarly eclectic mix of locals, while there's some excellent nightlife options on nearby rue de l'Église (Map p114, B2). For a dynamic slice of contemporary Québec City, take a stroll, heading 1km west, outside the old quarters.

Champlain set up his 'Habitation,' a small stockade, 80 years prior to the church's arrival.

☉ FORTIFICATIONS OF QUÉBEC

Map p111; ☎ 418-648-7016, 800-463-6769; 100 rue St-Louis; admission to interpretive center $4; ☽ 10am-5pm May-Oct; 🚌 3, 11
These largely restored old walls are a national historic site. You can walk the complete 4.6km circuit above the Old Town for free. There's also an interpretive center describing the history of the fort.

☉ LA CITADELLE

Map p111; ☎ 418-694-2815; www .lacitadelle.qc.ca; 201 Côte de la Citadelle; admission $10; ☽ 10am-4pm Apr & Sep, 9am-5pm May & Jun, 9am-6pm Jul & Aug, 10am-3pm Oct, closed Nov-Mar; 🚌 3, 11
A visit to this massive star-shaped fort above the St-Lawrence River

is a must for understanding the strategic importance (and raison d'être) of Québec City. Hour-long guided tours give you an inside look at the old buildings. The changing of the guard takes place at 10am daily in the summer months.

☉ MUSÉE DE LA CIVILISATION

Map p111; ☎ 418-643-2158; www.mcq .org; 85 rue Dalhousie; admission $11, free Tue Nov-May 31; ☽ 9:30am-6:30pm late Jun-early Sep, 10am-5pm Tue-Sun early Sep-late Jun
One of the biggest and best museums in Québec City, the Musée de la Civilisation houses fascinating multimedia exhibits covering the human history of the region from aboriginal cultures to the early days of separatism in the 1960s and on up to the present day.

ST ROCH & ST JEAN-BAPTISTE

◉ MUSÉE DU FORT

**Map p111; ☎ 418-692-1759; 210 rue
Ste-Anne; admission $8; ⏱ 10am-5pm
Apr-Oct, 11am-4pm Thu-Sun Nov, Feb &
Mar; 🚌 3, 7, 11**
Not really a museum at all, the
Musée du Fort houses a 30-minute
multimedia show on the many
attempts over the centuries to
take Québec City. Although a bit
hokey, the show does give a good
introduction to the city's history.

◉ MUSÉE NATIONAL DES BEAUX-ARTS DU QUÉBEC

**Map p114; ☎ 866-220-2150; www.mnba
.qc.ca; Battlefields Park; permanent collection free, temporary exhibitions admission
$15; ⏱ 10am-6pm Thu-Tue & to 9pm Wed
Jun 1-early Sep, to 5pm Tue & Thu-Sun & to
9pm Wed late Sep-May; 🚌 11**
Spread among three impressive
buildings, the Musée National is
one of the gems of the Canadian art world – and contains

the world's largest collection of
Québec art (some 34,000 pieces).
Highlights of the permanent col-
lection include works by Jean-Paul
Lemieux (1904–90) and Jean-Paul
Riopelle (1923–2002) as well as an
extensive Inuit art collection. See
p19 for more.

◉ OBSERVATOIRE DE LA CAPITALE

**Map p114; ☎ 418-644-9841; 1037 rue
de la Chevrotière, Édifice Marie-Guyart;
admission $5; ⏱ 10am-5pm Tue-Sun;
🚌 11, 25, 28**
Head 221m up to the 31st floor
for great views of the Old Town,
the St-Lawrence River and (if it's
clear enough) even the Laurentian
Mountains.

◉ PARC DES CHAMPS DE BATAILLE (BATTLEFIELDS PARK)

**Map p114; ☎ 418-648-3506; www.ccbn
-nbc.gc.ca; day pass $10; ⏱ 10am-5pm;
🚌 3, 11**

This park contains the Plains of Abraham, setting of the infamous 1759 battle between British General James Wolfe and French General Montcalm that determined the fate of the fledgling colony. The area is packed with historic sites; day passes give free admission to key locales. The park also has a nature trail as well as a jogging track – come winter it brings snowshoeing and cross-country skiing.

DO

CROISIÉRES AML River Cruise

Map p111; ☎ 866-856-6668; www .croisieresaml.com; Quai Chouinard, Vieux-Port; 1½hr cruise $32

AML runs several popular cruises, including a 90-minute sightseeing excursion around the St-Lawrence (with historical commentary provided by costumed guides) and two-hour weekend brunch cruises.

SHOP

CHOCO-MUSÉE Chocolate

Map p114; ☎ 418-524-2122; www.choco musee.com; 634 rue St-Jean; 🕑 10am-5:30pm Sat-Wed, to 9pm Thu & Fri

Heavenly scents and gustatory temptations of all shapes and flavors await visitors who enter the Choco-Musée. In addition to exotic berry ice creams and strawberry-and-basil truffles, there's a little

museum out the back where you can watch the chocolatiers work.

LA PETITE CABANE A SUCRE DU QUÉBEC Food

Map p111; ☎ 418-692-5875; 94, rue du Petit-Champlain; 🕑 10am-5:30pm Sat & Mon-Wed, 10am-9pm Thu & Fri, 11am-5:30pm Sun

Maple syrup is a massive industry in Québec, and this little shop sells it in every shape and form: candies, delicacies, ice-cream, snacks, syrup-related accessories and, of course, the sweet stuff straight up.

MARCHÉ DU VIEUX-PORT Food

Map p111; ☎ 418-692-2517; 160 Quai St-André; 🕑 9am-5pm

This is a local market where you can buy fresh fruits and vegetables as well as dozens of local specialties, from Île d'Orléans blackcurrant wine to ciders, honeys, chocolates and, of course, maple-syrup products.

SILLONS CDs

Map p114; ☎ 418-524-8352; 1149 av Cartier; 🕑 10am-9pm Mon-Fri, 10am-5pm Sat, 11am-5pm Sun

This longtime independent record store specializes in jazz, world music and sounds from Québec and France. It's a great place for advice on the latest hits from the francophone world.

FAIRMONT LE CHÂTEAU FRONTENAC
Map p111; ☎ 418-692-1751; 1 rue des Carrières

More than just a hotel or a landmark, the castlelike Château Frontenac is the enduring symbol of Québec City. Designed by New Yorker Bruce Price, the Château was named after the mercurial Count of Frontenac, Louis de Buade, who governed New France in the late 1600s. Completed in 1893, Château Frontenac was one of the Canadian Pacific Railway's series of luxury hotels built across Canada. One part medieval and one part Renaissance, the hotel has had regular extensions over the years, the most recent in 1993.

Its turrets and dramatic facade loom high above Cap Diamant, atop a cliff that swoops down into the St-Lawrence River. The setting alone is so powerful that Alfred Hitchcock opened his 1953 Québec City–set mystery, *I Confess*, with that very shot.

During WWII, the Québec Conferences involving British prime minister Winston Churchill, US president Franklin Roosevelt and Canadian prime minister William Lyon Mackenzie King were all held here.

Guides in period costume give **50-minute tours** (☎ 418-691-2166; www.tours chateau.ca) on the hotel's history. Call for reservations.

THE ICE HOTEL

Visiting North America's first ice hotel, which opened in 2001, is like stepping into a wintry fairy-tale. Nearly everything here is made of ice: the reception desk, the pen with which you sign in, the sink in your room, your bed, even the cocktail glasses – all ice.

Some 500 tons of ice and 15,000 tons of snow go into the five-week construction of this perishable hotel. One of the most striking aspects is its size – over 3000 sq meters of frosty splendor. First impressions in the entrance hall are strangely overwhelming – tall, sculpted columns of ice support a ceiling where a crystal chandelier hangs, and carved sculptures, tables and chairs line the endless corridors.

The hotel lies about a half-hour drive from central Québec City. Packages at the **Ice Hotel** (www.icehotel-canada.com) start at $320 per double, though you can also stop in for a tour ($16).

EAT

AUX ANCIENS CANADIENS
Québécois $$$

Map p111; ☎ 418-692-1627; www.aux ancienscanadiens.qc.ca; 34 rue St-Louis; mains $22-36; ☽ noon-9pm

Housed in the historic Jacquet House, which dates from 1676, this place is all about robust country cooking and typical québécois specialties. Wait staff in historic garb serve dishes like caribou in blueberry wine sauce, grilled pheasant and braised duckling in maple-syrup sauce. For the best value, go at lunchtime.

CASSE-CRÊPE BRETON
Creperie $

Map p111; ☎ 418-692-0438; 1136 rue St-Jean; mains under $7; ☽ 8am-6pm

Tiny and unassuming, this welcome spot specializes in hot, fresh crepes of every kind, starting as low as $4. Some diners like to sit at the counter and watch the chef at work.

CHEZ TEMPOREL *Cafe* $

Map p111; ☎ 418-694-1813; 25 rue Couillard; mains $6-10; ☽ 7am-midnight

This cafe serves tasty sandwiches, homemade soups and quiches, plus prodigious salads, fresh baked goods and excellent coffees. Despite the great old-town location, it attracts a mostly local crowd.

LAURIE RAPHAËL
French, Québécois $$$

Map p111; ☎ 418-692-4555; 17 rue Dalhousie; mains $38-54; ☽ 11:30am-2pm Tue-Fri, 6-10pm Tue-Sat

This highly respected restaurant features a blend of *produits du terroir* (local Québec produce), along with international accents. Delectable favorites include giant scallops with coconut milk and exotic fruits and lamb with mint and anise. There's also a spontaneous chef's menu ($60) 'for those that like to be surprised.'

LE 48 *International* $$

Map p111; ☎ 418-694-4448; 48 rue St-Paul; mains $14-20

This stylish spot leans toward theatricality with its sleek black tables and chairs and Cirque du Soleil footage playing in the background. The menu features tasty global bistro fare (Asian noodle soups, gourmet burgers, salads, pizzas) and there's an outdoor patio.

LE CAFÉ DU CLOCHER PENCHÉ *French Bistro* $$

Map p114; ☎ 418-640-0597; 203 rue St-Joseph Est; brunch around $16, mains $23-29; ☽ 8am-11pm Mon-Fri, from 11am Sat & Sun

Well worth making the trip outside the old town, this classic restaurant prepares creative bistro fare and proudly serves local products such as Québec cheeses. It also has a superb weekend brunch (reservations essential).

🍴 LE COCHON DINGUE
Cafe $$

Map p111; ☎ 418-692-2013; 46 blvd Champlain; mains $10-12; ⏰ 8am-1am
This longtime favorite serves unfussy bistro fare in a casual setting. There's nicely prepared cafe au lait, *croque monsieur,* sandwiches, salads, mussels or quiche. Grab an outside seat in warm weather and watch the crowds shuffling by.

🍴 L'ÉCHAUDÉ *Bistro* $$

Map p111; ☎ 418-692-1299; 73 rue Sault-au-Matelot; mains $18-29; ⏰ 11:30am-2:30pm Mon-Fri, also 6pm-late daily, brunch 10am-2:30pm Sun
A handsome and relaxed neighborhood spot, L'Échaudé is one of the nicest bistros in the Old Town, and attracts as many locals as tourists. Top dishes include braised lamb, risotto, *steak frites* and a rich mussel and fish soup.

🍴 PAILLARD CAFÉ-BOULANGERIE
Bakery, Sandwiches $

Map p111; ☎ 418-692-1221; 1097 rue St-Jean; mains $7-9; ⏰ 7:30am-7pm
This bright and buzzy space has high ceilings, huge bay windows and long wooden tables where diners tuck into tasty gourmet sandwiches, satisfying soups and fresh salads. The attached bakery spreads decadent desserts.

🍸 DRINK

🍸 LE SACRILÈGE *Bar*

Map p114; ☎ 418-649-1985; 447 rue St-Jean; ⏰ noon-3am
It's been around for over 10 years, but most night owls still start or end their weekend revelry at this watering hole. There's a popular terrace out the back – get to it through the bar or the tiny brick alley next door.

🍸 L'ONCLE ANTOINE *Bar*

Map p111; ☎ 418-694-9176; 29 rue St-Pierre; ⏰ 11am-1am, to 3am Fri & Sat
Set clandestinely in the stone cave-cellar of one of the city's oldest surviving houses (dating from 1754), this great tavern pours out excellent Québec microbrews, several drafts and various European beers.

🍸 PUB ST-ALEXANDRE *Bar*

Map p111; ☎ 418-694-0015; 1087 rue St-Jean; ⏰ 11:30am-around 1am
High ceilings and dark wood set the scene at this popular watering hole. Tourists and locals alike come for the pub-like atmosphere and encyclopedic range of suds (250 sorts).

Wet your whistle at Pub St-Alexandre

STARRING QUÉBEC CITY

For a look at Québec City through the eyes of one of the world's great filmmakers, check out I Confess by Alfred Hitchcock (1953). The suspenseful film-noir-ish thriller is based on a French play about a priest grappling with his vows of silence after hearing a murderer's confession. Hitchcock was so taken with Québec City he based the entire story here and made the characters Canadian.

A few decades later, Robert Lepage, Québec City's most famous playwright and director, paid homage to the earlier film in Le Confessionnal (The Confessional, 1995). In it Lepage takes an unvarnished look at that moment in Québec City's history when Maurice Duplessis was premier of Québec (see p147), TV had made its first appearance and Hitchcock was arriving in town. Sometimes retracing Hitchcock's steps, Lepage creates a complex and captivating portrait of Québec City.

⭐ PLAY

⭐ BOUDOIR LOUNGE
Club

Map p114; ☎ 418-524-2777; 441 rue de l'Église, St-Roch; ☽ noon-3am
One of St-Roch's trendiest nightclubs, this spacious, handsomely designed club has two bars located upstairs and a disco held down below. In addition to DJ nights, there's live jazz and rock, salsa and other events. Cool off on the outdoor terrace in the summer.

⭐ GHOST TOURS OF QUÉBEC
Walking Tour

Map p111; ☎ 418-692-9770; www .ghosttoursofquebec.com; 4 1/2 rue d'Auteuil; tour $18; ☽ 8pm May-Oct
Local theater actors lead you through the dark streets of the Old Town by lantern as

they recount the hangings and hauntings of Old Québec. The 90-minute tours are great fun and they usually conclude with a visit to the city's most haunted building.

⭐ LE DRAGUE Club
Map p114; ☎ 418-649-7212; 815 rue Ste-Augustine; ☽ 10am-late
The star player on the city's tiny gay scene, Le Drague is made up of several sections – there is a front outdoor terrace, a two-level disco where the drag shows are held, a slightly more laid-back tavern, and the men-only revelry in Base 3.

⭐ LE GRAND THÉÂTRE DE QUÉBEC Performing Arts
Map p114; ☎ 877-643-8131; www .grandtheatre.qc.ca; 269 blvd René-Lévesque Est

The city's main performing arts center has a steady line up of top-quality classical concerts, dance and theater. The world-class **Opéra de Québec** (www.operadequebec.qc.ca) also performs here.

⭐ **LES VOÛTES DE NAPOLÉON**
Live Music
Map p114; ☎ **418-640-9388; 680A Grande-Allée;** ⏲ **7pm-1am**
One of the city's best-loved *boîte à chansons* (Québec folk-music clubs), lies underneath the Restaurant Bonaparte (it's difficult to find), and makes for a deliciously authentic evening of song.

Montréal and Québec City have their subcultures – and they are many. No matter your interest, you can pursue it with abandon in these free-spirited cities. For insight into cutting-edge boutiques, québécois cuisine, the underground club scene, cinema and performing arts, traveling with kids and much more, read on.

Le St-Sulpice (p75), Quartier Latin

ACCOMMODATIONS

Montréal and Québec City are blessed with a great variety of accommodations, from the plush and stylish to the minimalist and economical. Though rates aren't cheap, they are reasonable by international standards – or even compared to Canadian cities such as Toronto or Vancouver. French- and Victorian-style inns and independent hotels cater to a variety of budgets.

The B&B is one of Montréal's strong suits. Many of them are set in attractive, 19th-century stone houses close to the Plateau's bar-and-restaurant strips of blvd St-Laurent and rue St-Denis, or near rue Ste-Catherine Est in the Village. Small, European-style hotels are another local specialty. Located downtown and in the Quartier Latin, they occupy Victorian-era homes that are plain and functional or comfy and charming.

Old Montréal has the most atmospheric and most expensive digs in town. Over the last decade, many of the area's old buildings have been converted into boutique hotels with unique ambience and confident service.

Downtown is the bastion of the business hotel and the large upper-end chain. There are some interesting independent and budget hotels throughout the area. Most of the B&Bs are in the residential areas around McGill.

The student hub of Quartier Latin has decent places to stay close to the bars. Gay travelers often opt for guesthouses in the Village, with its delightful, superb-quality B&Bs. The Village is also so central and well served by métro lines that it's one of the best locations in the city to base yourself.

Staying in the fashionable district of the Plateau means being close to some of the best eateries and nightlife in town. Like the Village, the Plateau is sprinkled with atmospheric B&Bs; hotels are few and far between.

---

lonely planet Hotels & Hostels

Need a place to stay? Find and book it at lonelyplanet.com. Over 170 properties are featured for Montréal and Québec City – each personally visited, thoroughly reviewed and happily recommended by a Lonely Planet author. From hostels to high-end hotels, we've hunted out the places that will bring you unique and special experiences. Read independent reviews by authors and other travelers, and get practical information including amenities, maps and photos. Then reserve your room simply and securely via Hotels & Hostels – our online booking service. It's all at lonelyplanet.com/hotels.

From B&Bs to plush boutique hotels, Québec City has an enticing array of sleeping options. The best choices are the small European-style hotels and Victorian B&Bs around Old Town. They offer character and convenience.

Planning in advance is key to finding accommodations during big events. This is essential during key festivals such as the Montréal Jazz Festival (late June to early July) and the Québec City Summer Festival (mid July). Prices rise in the high-season summer months. In the off-season (October to April), rates can be 20% to 30% lower, except over Christmas and New Year.

You can book accommodation online through Québec's official tourism organization (www.bonjourquebec.com) for both Montréal and Québec City. You can also book B&Bs online at BB Select (www.bb.select .com) and BB Canada (www.bbcanada.com).

BEST PENNY PINCHERS

> Alternative Backpackers, Old Montréal (www.auberge-alternative.qc.ca)
> Hotel l'Abri Voyageur, Downtown (www.abri-voyageur.ca)
> Auberge Maeva, Plateau du Mont Royal (www.aubergemaeva.com)
> Le Sous-Bois, Old Montréal (www .lesousbois.com)
> HI Montréal, Downtown (www .hostellingmontreal.com)

MOST ATMOSPHERIC B&BS

> Le Petit Prince, Downtown (www .montrealbandb.com)
> Les Passants du Sans Soucy, Old Montréal (www.lesanssoucy.com)
> Petit Auberge Le Bons Matins, Downtown (www.bonsmatins.com)
> La Loggia, the Village (www.laloggia .ca)
> Anne Ma Soeur Anne, Plateau du Mont Royal (www.annemasoeuranne .com)

MOST STYLISH HOTELS

> Hotel Nelligan, Old Montréal (www .hotelnelligan.com)
> Auberge du Vieux-Port, Old Montréal (www.aubergeduvieuxport.com)
> Hôtel Place-d'Armes, Old Montréal (www.hotelplacedarmes.com)
> Hotel Kutuma, Plateau du Mont Royal (www.kutuma.com)
> Hotel Gault, Old Montréal (www .hotelgault.com)

BEST QUÉBEC CITY SLEEPS

> Fairmont Le Château Frontenac (www.fairmont.com)
> Hotel Maison du Fort (www.hotel maisondufort.com)
> Auberge Saint Antoine (www.saint -antoine.com)
> Le Clos Saint-Louis (www.clossaint louis.com)
> Auberge JA Moisan (www.jamoisan .com)

FOOD

Montréal has rich culinary traditions, with an outstanding assortment of classic French cuisine, hearty québécois fare and countless ethnic restaurants from 80-odd nationalities. Today's haute cuisine is as likely to be conjured up by talented young Italian, Japanese or British chefs as graduates from the Académie Culinaire du Québec.

Montrealers can enjoy an enormous variety of locally produced ingredients and delicacies: raw cheeses, foie gras, game and maple syrup (see the boxed text, p83), to name a few. The outdoor markets carry exotic foodstuffs that weren't available even a decade ago, alongside the tasty produce from local farms. Marché Atwater (p49) and Marché Jean Talon (p99) are the city's two biggest markets – and great places to assemble a picnic from Québec's rich produce.

Residents argue heatedly over which places serve the best of anything – chewy bagels, espresso, comfort soup, fluffy omelet or creamy cakes. Montréal smoked meat (see the boxed text, p86) and bagels, of course, have a formidable reputation that stretches across the country and is a constant source of friendly rivalry with New Yorkers. Top places to sample the goods include Schwartz's (p86), Montréal's undisputed king of the smoked-meat sandwich, and St-Viateur (p100), serving delicious old-fashioned bagels fresh from the wood-burning oven.

Traditional québécois cuisine is classic comfort food, heavy and centered on meat dishes. The fact that the ingredients are basic is said to be a historical legacy, as French settlers only had access to limited produce. Québec City may lack the range of invention typified by the Montréal dining scene, but it has no lack of classic québécois restaurants.

The stereotypical québécois meal tends to be a hearty, cholesterol-filled affair and might include stews with potatoes, carrots or turnips; game (caribou, duck, wild boar); or *tourtière* (meat pie). A favorite staple is *poutine* (fries smothered in cheese curds and gravy). To appease your sweet tooth, order *pudding chômeur* (literally, 'pudding for the unemployed'), a kind of sponge cake doused in a gooey brown-sugar sauce.

Other classic québécois dishes include *tourtière* – a meat pie usually made with pork and another meat like beef or veal together with celery and onions – and *pâté chinois* – a kind of shepherd's pie with a layer of beef or pork, a layer of creamed corn and a layer of mashed potatoes that is jazzed up through family variations, like a fourth layer sprinkled with cheddar or parmesan cheese. Should you desire to tackle your own *tourtière* at home, pick up the cookbook *A Taste of Québec* by Julian Armstrong.

Québécois pea soup is the yellow variety (not the green split-pea soup you'll find elsewhere in Canada) and is usually packed with ham or another type of pork.

There's a fine choice of French food in the city, with bistros and brasseries of all types and price ranges. Many of them incorporate the best of Québec's produce and market ingredients, and you'll find everything from no-nonsense French food to experimental takes on the classics.

Wherever you go, keep an eye out for the *table d'hôte,* a fixed-price meal – usually three or four courses – that can be a good way to sample the chef's top dishes of the day. Many restaurants post signs advertising *'apportez votre vin'* (bring your own wine). Unlike in the US, there's rarely a corkage fee, so take advantage. Pick up your tipple from an outlet of the government's alcohol retailer, SAQ (Societé des Alcools du Québec), or a *depanneur* (convenience store).

BEST QUÉBÉCOIS RESTAURANTS

> Joe Beef (p46)
> L'Orignal (p64)
> Toqué! (p66)
> Au Pied de Cochon (p83)
> Le Club Chasse et Peche (p64)

BEST INTERNATIONAL RESTAURANTS

> Pintxo (p85)
> L'Express (p85)
> Café Ferreira (p46)
> Il Mulino (p96)
> Garde-Manger (p63)

Above Tempting tasting plates at Marché Jean-Talon (p99)

ART

Québec's lush forests and icy winter landscapes have been inspiring landscape artists since the 19th century. Horatio Walker was known for his sentimental interpretations of Québec farm life such as *Oxen Drinking* (1899). Marc-Aurèle Fortin (1880–1972) became famous for his water-colors of Québec countryside, notably the treescapes of the Laurentian Mountains and Charlevoix. His portraits of majestic elms along Montréal avenues can be viewed inside the Musée d'Art Contemporain (p42).

William Brymner influenced an entire generation of painters as director of the Art Association of Montréal in the early 20th century. His forte was delicate human figures, interiors and landscapes in the glowing colors of romantic classicism. One of his pupils was Clarence Gagnon, who pro-duced subtle snowscapes and dazzling autumn scenes. Other key artists of the period included Adrien Hébert and Robert Pilot, usually identified by their snowy portraits of Montréal and Québec City.

In the 1940s the modern era of Canadian painting was ushered in by three leading figures: Paul-Émile Borduas, John Lyman and Alfred Pel-lan, who all worked closely together in Montréal. Borduas developed a radical style of surrealism that came to be identified with an alternative group called the Automatistes.

In 1948 Borduas drafted the manifest *Refus Global* (Global Refusal), which rejected the values of traditional landscape painting in favor of abstract art. The highly controversial document endorsed personal freedoms of expression while attacking state repressions and the domi-nant place of the church in Québec.

The most prolific of the Automatistes was Jean-Paul Riopelle (1923–2002). Though initially a surrealist, Riopelle soon produced softer abstracts called 'grand mosaics' – paintings created with a spatula with colors juxtaposed like a landscape viewed from an airplane. In the 1980s he abandoned conventional painting to work with aerosol sprays. His most renowned paintings are on permanent display at Montréal's Musée d'Art Contemporain and the Musée National des Beaux-Arts du Québec (p115) in Québec City.

Abstract painting has been an exciting field to follow in the past few years in Montréal. François Lacasse is a master in manipulating acrylic into new depths that evoke a strong sense of virtuality without the aid of computers. And lithograph artists like Elmyna Bouchard and Francine Simonin are getting attention throughout Canada and abroad.

Québec City has its own crop of distinguished artists, some of whom were clearly captivated by the grandeur of Québec City and its surrounding scenery. Jean-Paul Lemieux (1904–90) is one of Canada's most accomplished painters. Born in Québec City, he studied at L'Ecole des Beaux-Arts de Montréal and later in Paris. He is famous for his iconic paintings of Québec's endless landscapes and the people's relationship to it. Many of his paintings are influenced by the simple lines of folk art. There's an entire hall devoted to his art at the Musée National des Beaux-Arts du Québec, and it is well worth a visit.

Alfred Pellan (1906–88) also studied at the local École des Beaux-Arts before moving to Paris. He earned attention for his striking portraits, still life, figures and landscapes, before turning to surrealism in the 1940s.

Québec City has also attracted its share of *émigrée* artists. Cornelius Krieghoff (1815–72) was born in Amsterdam but was acclaimed for his compelling portraits of Quebecers and aboriginal residents such as the Wendats.

Francesco Iacurto was born in Montréal but moved to Québec City in 1938 and his acclaimed works are dominated by the town's streetscapes, landscapes and portrayals of Île d'Orléans.

Montréal and Québec City both have excellent museums and a growing number of galleries. You can also see art in some unlikely places, including colorful street art around the Plateau district and even underground in some métro stations.

BEST ART GALLERIES

> Galeries d'Art Contemporain du Belgo (p39)
> Parisian Laundry (p43)
> Galerie St-Dizier (p57)
> Yves Laroche Galerie d'Art (p59)
> Galerie Le Chariot (p57)

MOST ARTFUL MÉTRO STATIONS

> Berri-UQAM (Map p71, B3)
> Champ-de-Mars (Map p55, D2)
> Peel (Map pp40–1, E2)
> Place-des-Arts (Map pp40–1, G2)

DRINKING

Montrealers love to drink. Maybe it's the European influence or that classic French *joie de vivre* but this is a town where it's perfectly acceptable, even expected, to begin cocktail hour after work and continue well into the night.

On a sunny Friday afternoon, the *cinq-á-sept* (5pm-to-7pm) festive tradition often becomes *cinq-á*-last call. (Legal closing time is 3am and most establishments stay open until then.) In warm weather, the bars, cafes, pubs and terraces that line blvd St-Laurent and rue St-Denis, for example, are packed with friends enjoying each other's company and the city's charm over a glass of wine, beer or other festive libations. Come wintertime, Montrealers are undaunted by snowstorms and long, frigid nights. In fact, that's when there's not much else to do but find yourself a warm, cozy bar and drink and laugh the night away.

As for places to sip, the city is brimming with options, from grungy holes-in-the-wall to glamorous lounges. You'll find Irish pubs, artsy French watering holes, elegant wine bars, microbreweries, pool halls, student taverns, dance-happy bars, bohemian tea houses, European cafes, and everything in between. Many hip restaurants unofficially become bars after midnight or so, some even pushing aside tables to make room for the influx of revelers.

As in Europe, espresso coffee is big here, and most locals start the day with strong, espresso-based drinks at their neighborhood cafes – many of which roast their own beans, and fair trade and specialty blends are fairly common.

The legal drinking age in the province of Québec is 18. Bars must close at 3am, so last call is usually about 15 minutes prior. Generally, you're expected to tip your server or bartender the greater of 15% of your bill, or between $1 and $2 for each drink you order.

Québec City has a small but festive drinking scene. Bars in the Old Town can be fun but generally quite touristy. For a more local flavor, it's worth exploring the bar scene in the New Town neighborhood of St-Roch.

BEST BARS
> Pub Ste-Élisabeth (p51)
> Blizzarts (p86)
> Reservoir (p88)
> Plan B (p88)
> Burgundy Lion (p50)

BEST CAFES
> Laïka (p88)
> Café Olímpico (p101)
> Le Cagibi (p98)
> Le Club Social (p102)
> Chez José (p87)

Top left Take your pick from an impressive selection of beers on tap at Barouf (p86)

NIGHTLIFE

Montréal nightlife is the stuff of legends: a vibrant, exciting and ever-evolving scene on the cutting-edge of international trends. That's why touring bands and DJs rave about Montréal audiences: crowds aren't afraid to let loose and really get into the musical experience. At live shows, they hoot, holler, and sing along, and even in cooler-than-thou clubs, people get down and dirty on the dance floor.

Its worldwide party-town reputation may make Montréal a bachelor-party and frat-weekend destination, but beyond such mainstream titilla-tion is the real deal. From underground dance clubs to French hip-hop, dub reggae to break-beat; comedy shows to supper clubs and the still exciting Anglo indie rock so hyped in the recent past, Montréal after dark holds something for everyone. You just have to know where to look.

To plan your soiree, Montréal's weekly newspapers (*Hour, Montreal Mirror,* and the French-language *Voir*) are good places to start. All three report on nightlife happenings including club events, live music, film, theatre, comedy, spoken word, installation art, and hybrids of the above. Pick up event flyers stacked in cafes and clothing and record shops throughout the Plateau, Mile End and the Village. Check out websites and blogs like www.midnightpoutine.com, www.montrealstateofmind .com, www.33mag.com and www.nightlifemagazine.ca. But the best way to get the goods is simply, to ask around!

Social dancing, especially tango, has also found a home in Montréal, and burlesque is big as well, with cabaret shows and dance classes. And then there are the music festivals – not the big kahunas but the little guys: **Pop Montreal** (www.popmontreal.com), **Osheaga** (www.osheaga.com), and **Suoni del Popolo** (www.casadelpopolo.com), as well as big gay and lesbian festivals like **Divers/Cité** (www.diverscite.org) and **Black & Blue** (www.bbcm.org).

Whatever your pleasure, grab a power nap and be prepared to go all night – although clubs close at 3am, there's always an after party!

BEST NIGHTCLUBS
> Tokyo Bar (p91)
> Baldwin Barmacie (p102)
> SAT (p53)
> Parking Nightclub (p77)
> Stereo (p77)

BEST LIVE MUSIC SPOTS
> La Sala Rossa (p89)
> Café Campus (p89)
> House of Jazz (p52)
> Zoobizarre (p103)
> Parc du Mont-Royal (p79)

Top left Bistro à JoJo (p76), Quartier Latin

PARKS & GREEN SPACES

Parks and green spaces are an integral part of Montréal society and fulfill many roles: a meeting ground for friends fleeing cramped apartments, weekend playground for sports lovers and a natural sanctuary from the scourges of urban life, to name a few.

The Parc du Mont-Royal (p79) is the city's favorite recreation spot. The looming hill – er, mountain – is visible from nearly every part of town and offers peaceful walking paths, gorgeous views of Downtown and plenty of amusement (bicycling, bird-watching, duck feeding, running, hippie drum circles) for outdoor enthusiasts.

Another major draw is the Parc Jean Drapeau (p104), which stretches between two islands in the St-Lawrence. You can catch a boat there in the summer, or bike or métro there anytime. Though not as lush as Mont-Royal, it's a great spot for cycling, and the islands hold a number of worthwhile attractions (museums, an amusement park, a casino) – not to mention fine views of the city and watery scenery surrounding it.

Smaller parks lie scattered all across Montréal, meaning you're never far from a bit of green after some serious urban exploring. The Plateau du Mont Royal has some fine grassy expanses, including: the leafy Parc La-Fontaine (p79), the city's third-largest park; and the Carré St-Louis (p79), a shady, picturesque square that's a favorite spot for musicians.

Old Montréal also has its share of inviting open-air spaces, such as the waterfront Parc du Bassin-Bonsecours (p60), with its open-air cafe, pond for paddleboats (or ice-skaters in winter) and pretty river views. Near here lies the starting point for the bike-and-running path along the Canal de Lachine, which continues uninterrupted for 14.5km to the Lac St-Louis.

Québec City has made good use of its strategic position – and picturesque views – above the mouth of the St-Lawrence. There's an abundance of green space near the Citadelle (p113), and the adjoining Parc des Champs de Bataille (Battlefields Park; p115) is a favorite spot among Quebecers not only for its history but also for its lush setting. The area became an official park in 1908 and has been the site of many modern historical events as well; 'O Canada,' the Canadian national anthem written by Sir Adolphe Routhier with music by Calixa Lavallée, was sung for the first time here on June 24, 1880.

Top left Parc du Mont-Royal (p79)

OUTDOOR ACTIVITIES

No matter the season, Quebecers are an active bunch, out jogging, cycling and kayaking on warm summer days, with winter bringing ice-skating, cross-country skiing and pick-up hockey games on frozen lakes.

Montréal teems with cycling and skating paths. There are leafy paths throughout the Parc du Mont-Royal (p79). There's also a fine route extending nearly 15km from Old Montréal along the Canal de Lachine, past the Marché Atwater and out to the Lac St-Louis. Tables are scattered along the canalside park, a peaceful spot for a picnic. The canal is also a fine spot to go kayaking. Hire kayaks or take an introductory course from H2O Adventures (p44).

The Circuit Gilles-Villeneuve (p107) is the smoothest track in town for in-line skating and cycling. It's open and free to all. You can rent gear bikes and in-line skates at Ça Roule (p59) in Old Montréal or My Bicyclette (p44) near the Marché Atwater.

Ice-skating, not surprisingly, is quite popular in Montréal. You can skate year-round at Atrium Le 1000 (p43). In winter, the frozen lakes around the city become makeshift rinks. Lac des Castors in Parc du Mont-Royal is a favorite spot, as is Parc du Bassin-Bonsecours (p60) in the Old Port.

For an adrenaline rush, visitors can climb aboard one of Saute Mou-tons' jet boats (p61), and ride through the foaming white water of the Lachine Rapids.

Québec City has some easily accessible opportunities for outdoor adventure. The pretty Parc des Champs de Bataille (Battlefields Park; p115) boasts a nature trail, footpaths, a jogging track and ideal spots for in-line skating. In winter, locals come here for snowshoeing, cross-country skiing or perhaps an evening sleigh ride.

Lac des Castors (p79), Parc du Mont-Royal

ARCHITECTURE

Montréal's split personality is nowhere more obvious than in its architecture: a beguiling mix of European classicism and North American modernity. Lovingly preserved Victorian mansions and stately beaux-arts monuments contrast with the sleek lines of modern skyscrapers. Sometimes one building even straddles the divide; the Centre Canadien d'Architecture (p39) integrates a graceful historical greystone right into its contemporary facade.

For many visitors, the weathered greystones, such as the old stone buildings along rue St-Paul (Map p111, C3), offer the strongest images of Old Montréal. The style emerged under the French regime in Québec (1608–1763), based on the Norman and Breton houses.

From the 19th century, some of Montréal's grandest buildings appeared, including the Gothic Basilique Notre-Dame (p56). In the early 20th century, French Second Empire style continued to be favored, and Montréal also boasts the largest collection of Victorian row houses in all of North America.

Other important buildings were meant to break with the past. Place Ville-Marie (p45), a multitowered complex built in the late 1950s, revolutionized urban architecture in Montréal. More radical forms emerged during the 1967 World's Fair in works such as: Habitat '67 (p106), a constructivist-style apartment building designed by Montréal architect Moshe Safdie; and Buckminster Fuller's Biosphère (p106), which once wore a skin made of spherical mesh.

Architectural highlights in Québec City are undoubtedly the soaring cathedrals and basilicas encompassing everything from Gothic to neoclassic elements. Québec's Old Town is also a brilliantly preserved relic of 18th-century New France.

Basilique Notre-Dame (p56), Old Montréal

CINEMA

The foundations of Québec cinema were laid in the 1930s when Maurice Proulx, a pioneer documentary filmmaker, charted the colonization of the gold-rich Abitibi region in northwestern Québec. It was only in the 1960s that directors were inspired by the likes of Federico Fellini or Jean-Luc Godard to experiment, though the subject of most films remained the countryside and rural life. The 1970s were another watershed moment when erotically charged movies sent the province a-twitter. One of the most representative works of this era was Claude Jutra's *Mon Oncle Antoine* (1971), a coming-of-age story set in Duplessis-era (see p147) rural Québec. Powerful themes echo in the film, not least of which is the social upheaval unfolding in the mining town where it is set – which presages the Quiet Revolution (see p148) to come. Some critics have hailed it as one of Canada's greatest films.

Montréal burst onto the international scene in the 1980s with a new generation of directors such as the celebrated Denys Arcand, whose themes struck a chord with international audiences. He tackled difficult subjects such as sexual liberation in *The Decline of the American Empire* (1986), religion in *Jésus of Montréal* (1989), and death in the brilliant *The Barbarian Invasions* (2003). The last touched on Québec's creaking healthcare system, the demise of the sexual revolution and the failed ideologies of the 1960s.

The city strongly supports independent and world cinema. For film buffs, the big event of the year is the Montréal World Film Festival (p28).

Eye-catching promotional posters for the Montréal World Film Festival (p28)

PERFORMING ARTS

Canada was a desert for playwrights in the early 1960s when a group of disgruntled writers formed the Playwrights' Workshop Montréal, which revolutionized the way plays were staged. An important drama center, the workshop has been the key to developing contemporary work and new writers for the Canadian stage. Its pioneers included playwrights such as Dan Daniels, Aviva Ravel, Walter Massey, Justice Rinfret and Guy Beaulne, many of whom are active on Montréal's theater scene today.

Founded in 1968, the Centaur Theater is Québec's premier English-language stage for drama. The main stage shows more mainstream fare, while a second stage features experimental theater.

Montréal's leading dance company is Les Grands Ballets Canadiens, which performs four shows annually – usually a mix of classical and modern pieces. Adding to the cultural fervor are numerous other troupes including Danièle Desnoyers' Le Carré des Lombes, Benoît Lachambre's Par b.l.eux and MAPS.

One of the biggest dance events of the year is the fairly new Festival Transamériques (p25), which features dozens of performances (some free) at theaters and outdoor venues all across town. It's held from late May to early June.

Québec's most famous brand is the internationally renowned Cirque du Soleil, which, since debuting in 1984, has set new artistic boundaries in its combination of dance, theater and circus performances. Before shows travel internationally, they are often staged first in Montréal under the Grand Chapiteau at the Old Port in early summer (see p67 and the boxed text, p67).

Tam-tam concert (p79) at Parc du Mont-Royal

GAY & LESBIAN MONTRÉAL & QUÉBEC CITY

Canada's most romantic metropolis doesn't just tolerate alternative life-styles – it hardly even bats an eyelash at them. Gay and lesbian marriage has been legal in Québec since 2004, and in many neighborhoods two women or men walking down the street and holding hands rarely gets a second look. The gay mecca of the city is the Village (p70), with its cafes, restaurants, sleek bars, galleries, sex shops and B&Bs – all irrepressibly adding to the city's open and free-spirited vibe. Here, no one cares if you speak English or French, what color you are, how you dress or who you sleep with. In fact, the appeal of mega-events like Divers/Cité (p27) is now mainstream, and some shows attract as many straights as gays. The other big event is the Black & Blue Festival (p28), which fills the Olympic Stadium for a mega-fest in early October.

Fugues is the free, French-language, monthly guide to the gay and lesbi-an scene for the province of Québec. It's an excellent place to find out about the latest and greatest naughty club or gay-friendly accommodations.

Québec City is a conservative town with a more village feel to it – open displays of affection between same-sex couples will attract a lot of atten-tion. There's a tiny but close-knit gay community centered on the club action at Le Drague (p122).

Vibrantly painted buildings in the Village (p70)

KIDS IN MONTRÉAL & QUÉBEC CITY

Montréal and Québec City provide plenty of entertainment for little ones.

Old Montréal (p54) with its lively street performers is a good place to wander – even better, save kids' legs with a ride atop a carriage (p60). Other good nearby options include high-speed jet-boat trips (p61) and more-leisurely boat cruises (p59).

La Ronde Amusement Park (p108) in Parc Jean-Drapeau will keep the kids entertained all day in summer. Another good bet is the Montréal Planetarium (p42). The Old Port offers many popular options, such as the Centre des Sciences de Montréal and its IMAX Cinema (p56). The abundance of bicycle paths weaving through green surrounds offers a great diversion for kids, especially along the Canal de Lachine from the Old Port (p58).

Québec City, with its old architecture, guides dressed in period costume and military attractions, is also packed with activities of interest to kids. A good place to begin the foray is the Old Town (Map p111) and Parc des Champs de Bataille (Battlefields Park; p115).

In the historic area, walking the Fortifications (p113) suits all ages. The Citadelle (p113) ceremonies, with uniformed soldiers beating the retreat, for example, are winners too. Place d'Armes (Map p111, C4) and Place-Royale (Map p111, D3), with their abundance of buskers, always delight children, as would a slow tour of Old Town in one of the horse-drawn calèche that you'll see in the streets.

Place Jacques-Cartier (p58)

SHOPPING

Montréal is Canada's unofficial fashion capital and many of the country's most talented and internationally successful designers have roots here. Gorgeous locally based lines to look for include Denis Gagnon, Nadya Toto, Marie Saint Pierre, YSO, and that from up-and-comer Travis Taddeo. True fashionistas should visit during Montréal Fashion Week (p25), which takes place every June and October to showcase new collections.

Even beyond fashion, Montréal is an ideal shopping city, full of goods you'll want to take home. From big international department stores to high-fashion designers, vintage-clothing boutiques to weird one-of-a-kind antique shops, used music and booksellers, chic home decor and more, you'll find the cream of the crop in this shopping paradise.

Since Montréal is also a walking city, strolling down any of its prime outdoor shopping strips is a perfect way to spend a sunny afternoon. Upscale rue St-Paul (Map p55, C2) in Old Montréal is full of art galleries, designer furnishings and clothing shops. The district's touristy streets also house souvenir shops selling maple-syrup T-shirts and random Canadiana. Busy rue Ste-Catherine (Map pp40–1, E3) in the heart of Downtown has all the big names, department stores and some specialty shops and local fashion boutiques. For antiques, head southwest to rue Notre-Dame Ouest (Map pp40–1, C5). The trendy Plateau (p79) and artsy Mile End (p94) is full of hip clothing and home-decor boutiques, many located on blvd St-Laurent and rue St-Denis. Blvd St-Laurent has lots of vintage shops. Prices and style quotient soar on av Laurier (Map p93; B6) and rue Bernard (Map p93; B4) in Outremont.

Bustling rue St-Paul, Old Montréal (p54)

Chapelle Notre-Dame-de-Bonsecours (p57), Old Montréal

BACKGROUND

HISTORY

Québec has had a tumultuous history, with both Montréal and Québec City experiencing a string of sparkling successes followed by dramatic downturns. Over the centuries Montréal has come from being the economic and political center of the Canadian universe, only to dissolve into a kind of national backwater.

EARLY HISTORY

The Island of Montréal was long inhabited by the St Lawrence Iroquois, one of the tribes who formed the Five Nations Confederacy of Iroquois. In 1535 French explorer Jacques Cartier visited the Iroquois village of Hochelaga (Place of the Beaver) on the slopes of Mont Royal, but by the time Samuel de Champlain founded Québec City in 1608, the settlement had vanished. In 1642 Paul de Chomedey de Maisonneuve founded the first permanent mission, despite fierce resistance from the Iroquois. Intended as a base for converting aboriginal people to Christianity, this settlement quickly became a major hub of the fur trade. Québec City became the capital of the French colony Nouvelle-France (New France), while Montréal's *voyageurs* (trappers) established a network of trading posts into the hinterland.

One of the major events that would dramatically impact the development of the colony occurred in 1759, just outside of Québec City, when British General James Wolfe won a decisive victory over the French. Canada forevermore would be in the hands of the British. After the conquest, Scottish fur traders consolidated their power by founding the North West Company.

The American army seized Montréal during the American Revolution (1763–1783) and set up headquarters at Château Ramezay. But even the formidable negotiating skills of Benjamin Franklin failed to convince French Quebecers (Québécois) to join their cause, and seven months later the revolutionaries fled empty-handed.

INDUSTRIAL REVOLUTION

In the early 19th century Montréal's fortunes dimmed as the fur trade shifted north to the Hudson Bay. However, a new class of international merchants and financiers soon emerged, founding the Bank of Montréal and investing in shipping as well as a new railway network. Tens of thousands of Irish immigrants came to work on the railways and in the factories, mills and breweries that sprang up along the Canal de Lachine. Canada's industrial revolution was born.

The Canadian Confederation of 1867 gave Quebecers a degree of control over their social and economic affairs and acknowledged French as an official language. French Canadians living in the rural areas flowed into the city to seek work and regained the majority. At this lofty point in its history, Montréal was Canada's premier railway center, financial hub and manufacturing powerhouse. The Canadian Pacific Railway opened its head office there in the 1880s, and Canadian grain bound for Europe was shipped through the port.

In the latter half of the century, a wave of immigrants from Italy, Spain, Germany, Eastern Europe and Russia gave Montréal a cosmopolitan flair that would remain unique in the province. By 1914 the metropolitan population exceeded 500,000 residents.

WAR, DEPRESSION & NATIONALISM

The peace that existed between the French and English ran aground after the outbreak of WWI. Many thousands of French Quebecers signed up for military service until Ontario passed a law in 1915 denigrating the status of francophones by restricting the use of French in schools. When Ottawa introduced the draft in 1917, French Canadian nationalists condemned it as a plot to reduce the francophone population. The conscription issue resurfaced in WWII, with 80% of francophones rejecting the draft while nearly as many English-speaking Canadians voted yes.

During the Prohibition era Montréal found a new calling as 'Sin City', when hordes of free-spending, pleasure-seeking Americans flooded over the border in search of booze, brothels and betting houses. But despite free-wheeling boom days, the good times didn't last. The Great Depression erupted in 1929, soon engulfing the entire country. Unemployment soared to 25% in 1933, while the Gross National Product fell by 40% between 1929 and 1939.

As the economy crumbled, Québec's nationalists turned inward with proposals to create cooperatives, nationalize the anglophone power companies and promote French-Canadian goods. Led by the right-wing, ruralist, ultraconservative Maurice Duplessis, the new Union Nationale party took advantage of the nationalist awakening to win provincial power in the 1936 elections. The party's influence would retard Québec's industrial and social progress until Duplessis died in 1959.

QUIET REVOLUTION

In 1960 the nationalist Liberal Party won control of the Québec assembly and passed sweeping measures that would shake Canada to its very foundations. In the first stage of what came to be known as the Quiet Revolution, the assembly created new public companies that employed huge numbers of people in industries like iron and steelworks, mining, petroleum extraction and forestry, and nationalized the provincial hydroelectric companies.

Suddenly francophones – who had long been denied equal rights in the private sector – were able to work in French and develop their skills in white-collar positions. Still, progress wasn't swift enough for radical nationalists, and by the mid-1960s they claimed Québec independence was the only way to ensure francophone rights.

To head off clashes with Québec's increasingly separatist leaders, prime minister Pierre Trudeau proposed two key measures in 1969: Canada was to be made fully bilingual to give francophones equal access to national institutions; and the constitution was to be amended to guarantee francophone rights. Ottawa then pumped cash into French–English projects which, nonetheless, failed to convince francophones that French would become the primary language of work in Québec.

In 1976 this lingering discontent helped René Lévesque and his Parti Québécois, committed to the goal of independence for the province, get elected. The following year the Québec assembly passed Bill 101, which made French the sole official language of Québec and stipulated that all immigrants enroll their children in French-language schools. The previous trickle of anglophone refugees turned into a flood. Alliance Québec, an English rights group, estimates that between 300,000 and 400,000 anglos left Québec during that period.

The Quiet Revolution heightened tensions not only in Québec but across Canada. After their re-election in 1980, federal Liberals, led by Pierre Trudeau, sold most Quebecers on the idea of greater rights through constitutional change, helping to defeat a referendum on Québec sovereignty by a comfortable margin. Québec premier Robert Bourassa then agreed to a constitution-led solution – but only if Québec was recognized as a 'distinct society' with special rights. In 1987 the federal Conservative Party led by prime minister Brian Mulroney unveiled an accord that met most of Québec's demands. The accord, however, was defeated, triggering a major political crisis in Canada. The failure to appease the separatists sealed the fate of Mulroney, who stepped down as prime minister in 1993, and of Bourassa, who left political life a broken man.

REFERENDUM & REBIRTH

In the early 1990s Montréal was wracked by political uncertainty and economic decline. No one disputed that the city was ailing. The symptoms were everywhere: corporate offices closed down and moved their headquarters to other parts of Canada, shuttered shops lined downtown streets, and derelict factories and refineries rusted on the perimeter. Relations between anglophones and francophones plumbed new depths after Québec was denied a special status in Canada.

The victory of the separatist Parti Québécois in the 1994 provincial elections signaled the arrival of another crisis. Support for an independent Québec rekindled, and a referendum on sovereignty was called the following year. While it first appeared the referendum would fail by a significant margin, the outcome was a real cliff-hanger: Quebecers decided by 52,000 votes – a razor-thin majority of less than 1% – to remain part of Canada. In Montréal, where the bulk of Québec's anglophones and immigrants live, more than two-thirds voted against sovereignty, causing Parti Québécois leader Jacques Parizeau to (in)famously declare that 'money and the ethnic vote' had robbed Québec of its independence.

In the aftermath of the vote, the locomotives of the Quiet Revolution – economic inferiority and linguistic insecurity among francophones – ran out of steam. Exhausted by decades of separatist wrangling, most Montrealers put aside their differences and went back to work.

Oddly enough, a natural disaster also played a key role in bringing the communities together. In 1998 a freak ice storm – some blame extra-moist El Niño winds, others blame global warming – broke power masts across the province like matchsticks, leaving over three million people without power and key services in the middle of a Montréal winter. Some people endured weeks without electricity and heat but regional and political differences were forgotten as money, clothing and offers of personal help poured into the stricken areas. Montrealers recount those dark days with a touch of mutual respect.

As the political climate brightened, Montréal began to emerge from a fundamental reshaping of the local economy. The city experienced a burst of activity as sectors like software, aerospace, telecommunications and pharmaceuticals replaced rust-belt industries like textiles and refining. Québec's moderate wages became an asset to manufacturers seeking qualified, affordable labor, and foreign investment began to flow more freely. Tax dollars were used to recast Montréal as a new-media hub, encouraging dozens of multimedia firms to settle in the Old Port area.

The result is a city transformed and brimming with self-confidence. Rue Ste-Catherine teems with trendy boutiques and department stores; Old Montréal buzzes with fancy hotels and restaurants; once-empty warehouses around town have been converted to chic apartments and offices. The Plateau has become one of North America's hippest neighborhoods.

Montréal's renewed vigor has lured back some of the anglophones who'd left in the 1980s and '90s. Language conflicts have slipped into the background because most young Montrealers are at least bilingual, and for the first time there are more homeowners than renters and property prices have soared. It's also one of the least divisive times in Montréal's history.

CULTURE & SOCIETY

Montrealers have one foot in Europe and the other in North America, giving the city a complex local culture. Montréal is often defined by its French and English characteristics, though the city is so much more than that. Other communities have made enormous contributions to the Montréal identity – notably its Italian, Greek, Haitian, Jewish, Portuguese and Lebanese immigrants.

On any given summer evening, streets around the Portuguese church in the Plateau may be closed off for a religious procession, while in Mile End a family of Hasidic Jews will be making their way to the synagogue. Further north, the sound of European football matches spill out of tiny trattorias in Little Italy. In fact, Italians now form the third-largest group in Montréal at more than 230,000, or more than 10% of the population.

These days the typical Montrealer embraces all the identities that make up the city – the nationalist St Jean-Baptiste society invites non-francophone groups to participate in the Fête Nationale, while anglophones have accepted French as the day-to-day language of Québec society, along with the realization that it's not the end of the world.

Not too long ago, if Montréal was in the national news, the topic probably had something to do with French–English struggles. These days, the city, and Québec in general, are more preoccupied with quite different societal concerns – like the high taxes citizens pay, the state of health care and the many roads in poor repair.

Compared to the rest of Canada, Quebecers are the staunchest supporters of gun control and environmental initiatives like the Kyoto accord, and they're the most opposed to the Canadian military's involvement in Afghanistan. Montrealers under 40 are also some of the least likely to marry and, anecdotally at least, more likely to be living together and raising children in common-law relationships.

The city is not without its share of challenges. There's a critical shortage of family doctors, meaning many Montrealers have no primary-care physician; and a law requiring parents to send their children to French public schools unless they themselves were educated in English, is controversial, as many families, including francophone ones, would prefer to educate their children in English.

Québec City has a reputation for being square and conservative (at least from the Montréal perspective) and locals often refer to it as a 'village' – with equal parts affection and derision. The city is also known as a notoriously challenging place for people born outside of it to establish themselves in the long term. With a near-homogenous French Catholic background, community ties go way back.

LANGUAGE

French is the official language of Québec, and French Quebecers are passionate about it – seeing their language as the last line of defense against Anglo-Saxon culture. What makes Montréal unique in the province is the interface of English and French – a mix responsible for the city's dynamism as well as the root of many of its conflicts.

Until the 1970s it was the English minority (few of whom spoke French) who ran the businesses, held positions of power and accumulated wealth in Québec; a French Quebecer who went into a downtown store, more often than not, couldn't get service in his or her own language.

But as Québec's separatist movement rose, the Canadian government passed laws (in 1969) that required all federal services and public signs to appear in both languages. The separatists took things further and demanded the primacy of French in Québec, affirmed by the Parti Québécois with the passage of Bill 101 in 1977. Though there was much hand wringing, Bill 101 probably saved the French language from dying out in North America. If you're at a party with five anglophones and one francophone these days, chances are everyone will be speaking French, something that would have been rare 10 years ago.

These days some 68% of Montrealers speak French more often at home, versus 18% English and 14% some other language. Bilingualism is widespread, with over half of the city's population fluent in both French and English. In Québec City, francophones are far more dominant, with French being the mother tongue of over 90% of city residents.

Québec settlers were relatively cut off from France once they arrived in the New World, so the French you hear today in the province, known colloquially as Québécois, developed more or less independently from what was going on in France. The result is a rich local vocabulary, with its own idioms and sayings, and words used in everyday speech that haven't been spoken in France since the 1800s.

Accents vary widely across the province, but all are characterized by a delicious twang and rhythmic bounce unique to Québec French. To francophone Quebecers, the French spoken in France sounds stilted. To people from France, the French spoken in Québec sounds old-fashioned, quaint and at times unintelligible – an attitude that ruffles feathers here in an instant, as it's found to be condescending. For French novices, communicating can sometimes seem like a one-way street: if you speak French, locals will have no problem understanding you – it's you understanding them that will be the problem. Remember, even when French-language Québécois films play in France, they are shown with French subtitles.

DIRECTORY

TRANSPORTATION
ARRIVAL & DEPARTURE
AIR

In Montréal, most flights (aside from charter flights) arrive and depart from **Montreal-Trudeau Airport** (☎ 394-7377, 800-465-1213; www.admtl.com), 21km west of Downtown.

Québec City's airport is **Aéroport International Jean-Lesage de Québec** (☎ 418-640-2700; www.aeroportdequebec.com), 15km west of the center.

Montréal-Trudeau Airport

To reach the city by public transit, there are several options. **L'Aérobus** (☎ 514-631-1856; www.autobus.qc.ca) travels every 30 to 60 minutes, 24 hours a day between the airport and Downtown. Buses terminate at the **main bus station** (Station Centrale de l'Autobus; Map p71, B3; ☎ 842-2281; 505 blvd de Maisonneuve Est; M Berri-UQAM), from where a free minibus will ferry you to any downtown hotel. The 45-minute journey costs $16/26 for a one-way/return ticket.

A slightly longer but cheaper journey entails taking two buses and the métro. Take bus 204 Est to the bus transfer station at Gare Dorval (Dorval Train Station). Here you switch to bus 211 Est; get off at métro station Lionel-Groulx. Both buses run from 5am to 1am and the entire journey to town should take about an hour. To get to the airport from Downtown, reverse the journey ($2.75 one way).

Taxis charge a flat rate between the airport and Downtown of $38 (for other destinations, you pay the metered fare).

Aéroport International Jean-Lesage de Québec

Québec City's airport has no bus services to town. A taxi costs a flat fee of $33 to go into the city.

VISA

Visas are not required for visitors from the EU, Australia, Israel, Japan,

---

AIR TRAVEL ALTERNATIVES

To cut back on carbon emissions, there are some worthwhile (and less expensive) alternatives to flying:

> Train: **Amtrak** (www.amtrak.com) provides service between New York City and Montréal on its Adirondack line. The trip though slow (11 hours) passes through lovely scenery. **VIA Rail** (www.viarail.ca), Canada's vast rail network, links Montréal with cities all across the country.

> Bus: **Greyhound** (www.greyhound.com) and its Canadian equivalent **Greyhound Canada** (www.greyhound.ca) provide extensive service across North America. Buses from Boston and New York make regular departures to Montréal.

CLIMATE CHANGE & TRAVEL

Travel – especially air travel – is a significant contributor to global climate change. At Lonely Planet, we believe that all who travel have a responsibility to limit their personal impact. As a result, we have teamed with Rough Guides and other concerned industry partners to support Climate Care, which allows people to offset the greenhouse gases they are responsible for with contributions to energy-saving projects and other climate-friendly initiatives in the developing world. Lonely Planet offsets all staff and author travel.

For more information, turn to the responsible travel pages on www.lonelyplanet .com. For details on offsetting your carbon emissions and a carbon calculator, go to www .climatecare.org.

New Zealand or the US. You will need to get a visa if you are from South Africa, Taiwan, developing countries or certain parts of Eastern Europe. Visa requirements change frequently so it would be a good idea to check with the **Citizen and Immigration Canada call center** (☎ 888-242-2100; www.cic.gc.ca), or to touch base with your Canadian consulate.

GETTING AROUND

Both Montréal and Québec City have fairly compact city centers, making it easy to get around on foot. Montréal also has a métro system for connections between neighborhoods. In this book, the nearest métro station (M) is noted after each listing.

PUBLIC TRANSPORTATION
Montréal

Montréal has a modern and convenient bus and métro system which is run by **STM** (☎ 786-4636;

www.stm.info). The aging métro generally runs from 6am to midnight from Sunday to Thursday, and 6am to 1:30am on Friday and Saturday.

One ticket can get you anywhere in the city with a connecting bus or métro train. If you're switching between buses, or between bus and métro, you should get a free transfer slip, which is called a *correspondance*, from the driver; on the métro take one from the machines just past the turnstiles.

Tickets cost $2.75, but are cheaper by the half-dozen ($12.75). Buses take tickets or cash but drivers won't give change. There are also tourist passes for one day ($9) and three days ($17).

A map of the métro network is included on the pull-out map at the back of this book.

Québec City

A ride on a white-and-blue **RTC bus** (Réseau de Transport de la Capitale; ☎ 418-

627-2511; www.rtcquebec.ca) costs $2.60 with transfer privileges, or $6.45 for the day. Many buses serving the Old Town area stop at Place d'Youville (Map p111, A4) just outside the wall on Rue St-Jean. Bus 800 goes to Gare du Palais (Map p111, A2), the central long-distance bus and train station.

BICYCLE

Montréal is one of the most bike-friendly cities in North America, with over 350km of bicycle paths across the city. In 2009, the city unveiled **Bixi** (www.bixi.com), an extensive network of bike-renting stations around town. For short jaunts, it's great value (one-day/one-month subscription fee is $5/28, and bikes are free the first half hour, $1.50 for every half-hour thereafter). Visitors can also rent bikes and in-line skates from **Ça Roule** (p155) in Old Montréal and **My Bicyclette** (p155) near the Atwater market.

Québec City has some 70km of bike routes and paths, including a route along the St-Lawrence, which connects to paths along the Riviére St-Charles.

TAXI

Flag fall in both Montréal and Québec City is a standard $3.30 plus another $1.60 per kilometer. Try **Taxi Champlain** (☎ 514-273-2435) or **Taxi Co-Op** (☎ 514-725-9885). In Québec City the biggest company is **Taxi Coop Québec** (☎ 418-525-5191).

TRAVEL BETWEEN MONTRÉAL & QUÉBEC CITY

Québec City lies about 260km northeast of Montréal. Aside from renting a car, there are a number of handy ways to get between the cities.

> Train: **Via Rail** (☎ 888-842-7245; www.viarail.ca) has several trains daily going between Montréal's **Gare Centrale** (Map pp40-1, F4; ☎ 514-989-2626; 895 de la Gauchetiére; Ⓜ Bonaventure) and Québec City's **Gare du Palais** (Map p111, A2; ☎ 888-842-7245; 450 rue de la Gare-du-Palais). Prices for the 3½-hour journey start at $50/$100 for a one-way/return ticket.

> Bus: **Orléans Express** (☎ 888-999-3977; www.orleansexpress.com) and **Greyhound** (☎ 800-661-8747; www.greyhound.ca) have services that depart daily between Montréal's **main bus station** (Station Centrale de l'Autobus; Map p71, B3; ☎ 842-2281; 505 blvd de Maisonneuve Est; Ⓜ Berri-UQAM) and Québec City's **Gare du Palais** (Map p111, A2; ☎ 418-525-3000; 450 rue de la Gare-du-Palais). Prices for the journey (3¼ to 4½ hours) start at $53/$106 for a one-way/return ticket.

Transport Times Between Key Destinations

	Old Montréal	Downtown	Quartier Latin	Plateau du Mont Royal	Mile End	Little Italy	Parc du Mont-Royal
Old Montréal	n/a	W 15min	W 15min	W 30min; M 10min	W 50min; M15min	M 20min	W 35min
Downtown	W 15min	n/a	W 20min; M10min	W 25min; M 10min	M 15min	W 20min	W 30min
Quartier Latin	W15 min	W 20min; M10min	n/a	W 15min; M 10min	W 45min; M 10min	W 35min	W 40min
Plateau du Mont Royal	W 30min; M 10min	W 25min; M 10min	W 15min; M 10min	n/a	W 15min; M 10min	W35min; M 10min	W 15min
Mile End	W 45min; M 15min	W 40min; M 15min	W 35min; M 10min	W 15min; M 10min	n/a	W 30min; M 10min	W 25min
Little Italy	M 20min	M 15min	W 45min; M 10min	W 35min; M 10min	W 25min; M 10min	n/a	M 10min + W 20min
Parc du Mont-Royal	W 35min	W 30min	W 40min	W 15min	W 25min	M 10min + W 20min	n/a

* W = walk   M = métro

PRACTICALITIES
BUSINESS HOURS

Restaurants typically open from 11am to 2:30pm and from 5:30pm to 11pm; cafes serving breakfast may open at 8am or 9am. Many bars and pubs open from 11am (some open at 5pm) till midnight or 3am, the legal closing time. After-hours clubs keep the party going till 8am or so the next day (but no alcohol is served after 3am).

Most banks in Montréal and Québec City are open from 10am to 3pm Monday to Wednesday and Friday, and from 10am to 7pm Thursday. Post offices are open from 8am to 5pm Monday to Friday.

Shops generally open at 9am on weekdays, closing at 6pm Monday to Wednesday, with late night shopping until 9pm on Thursday and Friday. Weekend hours are generally 10am Saturday and noon Sunday, to 5pm. Supermarkets open from 8am to 11pm daily.

Operating hours for tourist sites are shortened outside of peak season (May to September); in Québec City, some attractions close down completely outside of peak periods.

ELECTRICITY

Canada, like the USA, operates on 110V, 60-cycle electric power. Plugs have two flat vertical prongs (the same as the USA and Mexico).

EMERGENCIES

When in doubt, call ☎ 0 and ask the operator for assistance.
Poison Centre ☎ 1800-463-5060
Police, ambulance, fire ☎ 911
Police (less urgent) ☎ 280-2222

HOLIDAYS

New Year's Day January 1
Good Friday & Easter Monday late March to mid-April
Victoria Day May 24 or nearest Monday
Jean-Baptiste Day June 24
Canada Day July 1
Labor Day first Monday in September
Canadian Thanksgiving second Monday in October
Remembrance Day November 11
Christmas Day December 25
Boxing Day December 26

INFORMATION & ORGANIZATIONS

Eat Well Montreal (www.eatwellmontreal.com) Restaurant reviews, with photos, plus comments from other readers.
Fagstein (blog.fagstein.com) Funny, irreverent look at what's happening around the city.
Midnight Poutine (www.midnightpoutine.ca) A highly readable blog covering music, art, film, restaurants and events in Montréal.
Montréal Clubs (www.montreal-clubs.com) Keeps a finger on the pulse of Montréal's latest and greatest dance and party spots.

Québec City Tourism (www.quebecregion.com) Useful tourism website for Québec City and surrounding regions.
Tourisme Montréal (www.tourisme-montreal.org) Helpful state-run site with info on neighborhoods, events and more.

INTERNET

A growing number of cafes offer free wi-fi access. Register for free access and view the 150-odd places where you can get online in Montréal at **Île Sans Fil** (www.ilesansfil.org).

For free wi-fi hotspots in Québec City, visit www.zapquebec.org.

MONEY

Prices quoted in this book are in Canadian dollars.

Accommodations are likely to be your biggest expense, with midrange lodging averaging around $140 per day. Add in meals and entertainment, and a single traveler can anticipate spending about $200 per day. It's possible to get by on less – budget travelers staying in hostels and eating cheaply can survive on $60 a day or so. At the high end, travelers can stay in boutique hotels, dine at excellent restaurants and not scrimp on nightlife and spend upwards of $400 per day.

See the inside front cover for approximate exchange rates, or consult current rates at www.xe.com.

TELEPHONE

The only foreign cell phones that will work in North America are tri-band models, operating on GSM 1900 and other frequencies. If you don't have one of these, your best bet may be to buy a prepaid one at a consumer electronics store. Most phones cost less than $125 including voicemail, some prepaid minutes and a rechargeable SIM card.

US residents traveling with their phone may have service (though they'll pay international roaming fees). Get in touch with your cellphone provider for details.

COUNTRY AND CITY CODES

Canada's country code is ☎ 1, the same as the US. The area code for the entire Island of Montréal is ☎ 514. Québec City's area code is ☎ 418. Both cities have converted to 10-digit phone numbers, meaning you have to dial the area code even if you are dialing from the same area code as the one you want to call.

USEFUL PHONE NUMBERS

Directory Assistance ☎ 411
Operator ☎ 0

TIPPING

In restaurants, leaving a 15% tip on the pretax bill is standard. Tipping is expected for bar service, too. Most Canadians leave about $1 per drink.

At hotels, tip bellhops about $1 to $2 per bag. Leaving a few dollars for the room cleaners is always a welcome gesture. Cab drivers, hairdressers and barbers also expect a tip, usually 10% to 15%.

TOURIST INFORMATION

Montréal and Québec province share a central phone service for **tourist information** (☎ in Canada & US 877-266-5687, from outside Canada & US 514-873-2015; www.tourism-montreal .org). The airports have information kiosks that open year-round. For Québec province info, covering Montréal, Québec City and many other areas, visit **Bonjour Québec** (www.bonjourquebec.com).

Centre Infotouriste (Map pp40-1, E3; 1001 rue Square-Dorchester; ⏰ 9am-6pm; Ⓜ Peel) Teems with information on all areas of Montréal and Québec. The center also has separate counters dedicated to national parks, car rental, boat trips and city tours. Hotel reservations are provided free of charge.
Old Montréal Tourist Office (Map p55, D2; 174 rue Notre-Dame Est; ⏰ 9am-7pm late Jun-early Oct, to 5pm rest of year; Ⓜ Champ-de-Mars) Just off bustling pl Jacques-Cartier, this little office is always humming but staff are extremely helpful.

In Québec City:
Centre Infotouriste (Map p111, C4; ☎ 649-2608, 800-363-7777; 12 rue Ste-Anne; ⏰ 8:30am-7:30pm late Jun-early Oct, 9am-5pm rest of year) Central location in Old Town.

Centre Infotouriste (Map p114, D4; ☎ 641-6290, 800-266-5687, ext 798; 835 av Wilfrid-Laurier; ⌚ 8:30am-7:30pm Jun-early Oct, 9am-5pm Mon-Thu & Sat & 9am-6pm Fri, 10am-4pm Sun rest of year) In Battlefields Park.

TRAVELERS WITH DISABILITIES

Most public buildings in Montréal – including tourist offices, major museums and attractions – are wheelchair accessible, and many restaurants and hotels also have facilities for the mobility-impaired. Métro stations are not wheelchair accessible. However, almost all major bus routes are now serviced by NOVA LFS buses adapted for wheelchairs. It's recommended that you consult the bus service's website (www.stm.info/English/bus/a-usager-aps.htm) if you are a first-time user, to check availability on your route and become familiar with the boarding procedure on the adapted buses. **Access to Travel** (www.accesstotravel.gc.ca) provides details of accessible transportation across Canada.

Kéroul (☎ 252-3104; www.keroul.qc.ca; 4545 av Pierre-de-Coubertin; Ⓜ Pie-IX) Located a few kilometers east of Plateau du Mont Royal near Olympic Park, publishes *Québec Accessible* ($20), listing 1000-plus hotels, restaurants and attractions in the province rated by accessibility. It also offers packages for disabled travelers going to Québec and Ontario.

VIA Rail (☎ 871-6000, 888-842-7733; www.viarail.com) Accommodates people in wheelchairs at 48 hours notice. Details are available at Via Rail offices at Montréal's Gare Centrale, Québec City's Gare du Palais and other Canadian train stations.

Buses in Québec City's public transit are not wheelchair accessible, though there are other services available for travelers with disabilities.

Transport Accessible du Québec (☎ 641-8294; www.taxibijjou.com; ⌚ 6am-midnight) Wheelchair-adapted vans available. Make reservations 24 hours in advance.

Transport Adapté du Québec Métro inc (☎ 687-2641; ☎ 7:30am-10.30pm) Has 20 wheelchair adapted minibuses that zip around Québec providing door-to-door service (per trip $2.60). Make reservations at least eight hours in advance of your trip.

>INDEX

See also separate subindexes for Do (p164), Drink (p165), Eat (p165), Play (p166), See (p166) and Shop (p167).

🏃 **DO**

Amusement Parks
La Ronde 108

Beaches
Plage des Îles 108

Boating
Croisiéres AML 116

Carriage Rides
Calèche 60

Cycling & Skating
Atrium Le 1000 43
Ça Roule 59

000 map pages